HISPANIC BIOGRAPHIES

FATHER JUNÍPERO SERRA

Founder of California Missions

Donna Genet

Enslow Publishers, Inc.

40 Industrial Road   PO Box 38
Box 398   Aldershot
Berkeley Heights, NJ 07922   Hants GU12 6BP
USA   UK

http://www.enslow.com

Library of Congress Cataloging-in-Publication Data

Genet, Donna.
      Father Junipero Serra : founder of California missions / Donna Genet.
         p. cm. — (Hispanic biographies)
      Includes bibliographical references and index.
      Summary: Traces the life of Father Junípero Serra from his childhood on the
Spanish island of Majorca, his duties and travels as a missionary, to his death in 1784
and his legacy of the "Golden Chain" of missions in California.
      ISBN 0-89490-762-X
      1. Serra, Junípero, 1713-1784—Juvenile literature. 2. Explorers—
California—Biography—Juvenile literature. 3. Explorers—Spain—Biography—
Juvenile literature. 4. Franciscans—California—Biography—Juvenile literature.
5. Franciscans—Missions—California—History—18th century—Juvenile literature.
6. Indians of North America—Missions—California—Juvenile literature.
7. California—History—To 1846—Juvenile literature. [1. Serra, Junípero,
1713-1784. 2. Explorers. 3. Indians of North America—Missions—California.
4. California—History—To 1846.] I. Title. II. Series.
F864.S44G46 1996
979.4'02'092—dc20
    [B]   95-40199
                                             CIP
                                           AC

Printed in the United States of America

10 9 8 7 6 5

Illustration Credits: Donna Genet, pp. 8, 11, 18, 39, 56, 66, 72, 75, 83, 90, 97, 110, 114, 117.

Cover Illustration: Donna Genet

CONTENTS

CHAPTER ONE

MIGUEL JOSÉ'S
DREAM

 The Kumeyaay tribe attacked Mission San Diego de Alcalá swiftly; more than six hundred Kumeyaays were involved. Three hundred men attacked the nearby Spanish *presidio* (fort). Three hundred others attacked the mission that had been founded in July 1769 by Father Junípero Serra.[1]

The Native Americans were angry at the mission for many reasons; most had to do with the behavior of the Spanish soldiers who lived at the nearby presidio. Some of the soldiers raped Kumeyaay women. During one such assault, three soldiers had attacked and killed two people. Also, the soldiers let their animals graze on Native American lands; this had resulted in the crops being destroyed. The soldiers had also arrested two Kumeyaay leaders, Carlos and Francisco, for stealing. In addition to their anger at the soldiers' actions, Kumeyaay leaders were upset at the mission priests, who wanted to change the entire Kumeyaay culture. They wanted to "civilize" them, to make them convert to the Roman Catholic religion, and to teach them Spanish customs.[2]

Father Serra was not at the San Diego mission when the Kumeyaays attacked. Serra, the president for all the missions that had been built, was in the mission headquarters at Carmel. Father Fuster, who was at San Diego de Alcalá and who survived the attack, wrote to Father Serra telling him what happened.

The Kumeyaays were led by Carlos, the chief of a nearby village. On the night of November 4, 1775, they surrounded the rooms of the Kumeyaays who lived at the mission, to prevent them from warning the priests. The attacking Kumeyaays went into the mission church and took from it statues, religious clothing, and other items. The women went into the mountains with the stolen goods. The Kumeyaays probably just wanted to steal mission goods, but the soldiers heard them and started shooting.

The mission priests, who had been sleeping in other rooms, heard the noise and woke up. Father Luis Jaime, one of the priests, greeted the Kumeyaays with the words, "Love God, my sons." The men grabbed him, took him outside, and ripped off his clothing. They beat him with their clubs and shot him with arrows.[3] Then they set fire to the soldiers' barracks. Father Vicente, another priest, managed to stop the fire by smothering the flames with his clothing. The soldiers killed many of the Kumeyaays, and three of the four soldiers who guarded the mission were hurt.

When the sun started to rise, the Kumeyaays left. The priests found the body of thirty-five-year-old Father Luis, "so disfigured that they hardly recognized him."[4] The priests were overcome with grief.

After Father Serra read the letter explaining what had happened, he ordered the mission, which had been almost entirely destroyed, rebuilt. His boyhood dream had been to become a missionary who served God in faraway places. He would not let the mission's destruction stop him from reaching his goal: to build a chain of missions along the California coast. The missions would bring the Roman Catholic religion to the natives, and the priests would teach them how to farm and live like Spanish people. Before he died at the age of seventy-one, Father Serra built nine missions; others built twelve more. The missions would form a "golden chain" that would lead to the beginning of California, a great and rich state.

The gardens at the Santa Bárbara mission. The Spanish
priests and the Native Americans who lived at the California
missions planted many varieties of trees and plants.

Father Serra's influence continues today. The missions introduced crops such as oranges, olives, and almonds, which are an important part of California's economy. Highways and railroads follow *El Camino Real* (the Royal Highway), the road that linked the missions. Some of the largest West Coast California cities began as missions or presidios: San Diego, Los Angeles, and San Francisco.

The story of how Father Serra achieved his goal begins in the small Spanish town of Petra, on the island of Mallorca, where a long-wanted baby boy was born to the Serra family.

MIGUEL JOSÉ BECOMES FATHER JUNÍPERO SERRA

Margarita and Antonio Serra were excited. Margarita had given birth on November 24, 1713, to a boy they named Miguel José. Their other babies had died. Holding her son in her arms, Margarita prayed, "Lord, may this child survive." Antonio nailed a laurel branch to the door of their house, to let their relatives and friends know that they had a baby boy.[1]

Miguel José was born in the village of Petra, on the Spanish island of Mallorca, which is located in the

This statue of Father Serra is located in Ventura, California. The city's mission, founded in 1782, is sixty miles north of Los Angeles.

Balearic Islands that belong to Spain. Petra was twenty-five miles from Palma, the capital. The people who lived on the island were very religious: There were around one hundred forty thousand people, three hundred churches, and five hundred priests. Men and women greeted each other with the words *"Amar a Dios!"* ("Let us love God!"). The Serra baby was baptized in San Pedro, the village church.[2]

Three years later, the Serras had another child, a girl named Juana. Miguel José and Juana were very close. As a sign of affection, he called her *Juanita* (little Juana).

Like most villagers, the Serra family lived simply. Antonio Serra was a farmer who sometimes worked in the village rock quarry. The house had four rooms, a storeroom, and an attic. It had a rough floor and only a few pieces of furniture. The overhead loft was used to store such foods as cheeses, hams, and sausages. Light came from a wick that burned in oil. In the yard behind the house, mules were kept in a small corral. The mules were used to farm the land to help the family make grapes into wine. Wine was an important product that the family could sell.[3]

Mallorca has a mild climate, good for growing many kinds of crops. So many foods grow there that it is called the Golden Isle. (Years later, California was named the Golden State.) The foods that the islanders ate were bread, beans, cheese, fruit, fish, and vegetables. They grew olives, figs, oranges, lemons, almonds, and artichokes. Sometimes they had *enseimada*, a sweet cake.[4]

Although Miguel José was small for his age, he had many responsibilities. He spent long hours working on the family farm, located some distance from the village. He also led the animals to pasture and carried a heavy water bucket from the village well to his house. Life was different then. The village had no running water, electricity, or inside toilets.

Although Antonio and Margarita could not read or write, they wanted their clever Miguel José to have a good education. As soon as he was old enough, they enrolled him in the local church school, San Bernardino. At the school, he learned reading, writing, church music, and simple math. He also studied religion and learned Latin, the language then used in church services, law, and medicine.

The priests who ran the school were members of the Franciscan religious order. The order was founded by St. Francis of Assisi, an Italian who lived from 1182 to 1226. The men who lived in the order devoted their lives to God. They agreed to give up all material wealth and to work only for God's glory. Members called each other brother. In Spanish, they were often called *fray*. In English, Franciscan brothers are called friars or sometimes fathers.

Miguel José wanted to be a priest from an early age. This goal probably made his parents and teachers happy, because he was a good student and he was very religious. He would be an excellent priest.

He had another goal that he told no one, not even his friends. What he really wanted to do was to become a missionary.[5] Missionaries did religious work all over the world. They worked hard, had little food, and were poor. Although their lives were difficult, they could achieve so much. They could convert native peoples to the Roman Catholic religion. They could bring them to God!

Miguel José wanted more than anything else to become a missionary. He wanted to travel thousands of miles to strange places where no other missionaries had been before. Like many of the other village children, he had heard stories told by the friars about famous missionaries.[6] To the children, the missionaries seemed as exciting as modern rock stars are now.

Miguel José was especially interested in visiting and working across the Atlantic Ocean in the Spanish-controlled lands called New Spain. Miguel had been told about St. Francis Solano who lived from 1549 to 1610. Father Solano was a missionary whom Miguel José greatly admired. St. Francis Solano traveled through a large area of land in what is today South America. He loved music and played the violin. His music attracted the attention of many Native Americans, who later decided to become Christians.

Miguel José loved this story as well as the others told by the friars. He wanted to start missionary work as soon as he could. Although he knew that he would miss his family, friends, and village, he was ready to go as soon as possible. He did not know that it would take him almost twenty years to start his journey.

Miguel José was such a good student that his parents and his teachers wanted him to receive more education than he could get in his village. Taking holy vows was one of the few ways in which children could further their education. After he turned fifteen, his parents took him to Palma, the Mallorcan capital, so that he could be enrolled in the university to get an education and then become a priest.

Palma was an old walled city that had sixty churches and thirty thousand people. It was small compared to a large modern city, but to Miguel José, who came from a small town of two thousand people, it must have seemed huge.

Before Miguel José could enter the Franciscan convent, he needed more study. His parents hired a canon, a priest who worked for the cathedral, to be his tutor. The canon would oversee his studies and religious work. The Serras returned to Petra, leaving their son with his tutor.

One year later, Miguel José became a philosophy student at the church school. A philosophy student studies the purpose and meaning of life as well as the role of human beings. The school, at the Convent of San Francisco, was named in honor of St. Francis of Assisi. It prepared students for many types of jobs, such as priests, teachers, and doctors. Miguel José studied at the convent for one year and then applied to enter the Franciscan religious order.

Although Miguel José was very bright, the priest in charge of the Franciscan convent refused to admit him because Miguel José, who was short, looked too young. The priest told Miguel José that he could not be admitted until he was older.[7]

Miguel José's tutor and other priest friends tried to convince the convent leader to let Miguel José enter the order. After they spoke to him about Miguel José's interest in becoming a priest, the convent leader changed his mind. Miguel José was allowed to enter the convent, located just outside the city walls. For the rest of his life, he wore the Franciscan habit, a hooded wool robe that is held in place by a rope cord.

In the convent, which was called Jesus-Without-the-Walls, his life was hard. He and all other new students who wanted to be priests had to complete a one-year probationary period. Each day, he spent between six and seven hours praying. He also was assigned work, but he was too small to do heavy chores. Instead, he cleaned the stables and scrubbed the floors. He also continued his regular studies. He must have felt lonely, because his family was not allowed to write or to visit him.[8]

During this year, he read a great deal about the Franciscan order. Its priests were known as gray friars because of the color of their undyed wool habits. Most of the Franciscan priests came from poor families. They served God in many places: Europe, the Middle East, Asia, and in the New World. They were expected to be honest, poor, and humble.[9]

Miguel José did well in his studies and liked his religious education. He also did his best with his work assignments. He had a good memory and a nice singing voice. Although all the men who were studying to be priests were assigned to turn the large sheepskin pages of the hymnbook used for religious songs, Miguel José could not. He was too short to reach it. He also was sickly. He wrote, "I was almost always ill and so small of stature that I was unable to reach the lectern."[10] As an adult, he grew to five feet, two inches; he weighed about one hundred ten pounds. The father in charge of the novices, the priests-in-training, gave him other duties.

Like every Franciscan novice, Miguel José read books about the life of St. Francis of Assisi and his early companions.[11] Miguel admired Brother Junípero, a devoted friend of St. Francis of Assisi. Brother Junípero was named for the strong juniper tree; he liked practical jokes and was known as the "jester of the Lord." Brother Junípero also was so religious that he tried to model his life after that of Jesus Christ. He was always good to others.[12]

This hymnbook is kept at the Santa Bárbara mission. The pages of the hymnbooks were usually made from sheepskin.

After his probation ended, in September 1737, Miguel José took the vows that were needed to become a priest. He promised never to marry, always to be poor, and to follow his superiors' orders. Following the Franciscan custom of taking the name of a Franciscan father, Miguel José took the name of Brother Junípero as his own. From that time on, he was often called Fray or Father Junípero Serra.

Father Serra felt that the day that he took his vows, an important step in becoming a priest, was one of the most important days of his life. Each year he renewed his vows; this was part of the Franciscan tradition. Father Francisco Palóu, a priest who later wrote about Father Serra's life, explained, "He never spoke of it [taking vows] without tears in his eyes."[13]

After he took vows, Father Serra left the convent to study at St. Francis, another convent in the center of Palma. He spent the next eighteen years there—six studying to become a priest and twelve teaching college students.[14]

The Church of San Francisco, the second largest in Palma, was built two hundred years before Columbus's New World trips. Father Serra studied in the convent's well-known university. To become a priest, he had to study many subjects. He did excellent academic work, and his superiors were pleased with his achievements. After passing his exams, he became a philosophy teacher. During this time, he was ordained as a priest and began to preach sermons. He loved books so much that he was appointed convent librarian.[15]

In his first philosophy class, Father Serra taught twenty-eight students. Two of them, Francisco Palóu and Juan Crespí, later worked with him and also became famous as California missionaries. Both were from Palma.

Not much is known about Father Serra's life during this time, but it is known that Father Serra was chosen by the university to give an important sermon in honor of the great scholar Ramón Llull. One professor who heard the sermon wrote, "This sermon is worthy of being printed in letters of gold."[16]

Although he greatly enjoyed his university and church work, Serra still had his childhood dream: to become a missionary. He was uneasy about telling his colleagues about his plans, but he did reveal his plans to his superior. There is no record of his superior's reactions.

When Fathers Serra and Palóu heard about a call for missionaries to travel to Mexico, they sent their request for the job to Franciscan headquarters in Madrid, Spain's capital. Unknown to them, their earlier similar request had been opened and torn up. Father Serra was such a good teacher that the convent officials did not want him to leave.

If they were allowed to become Mexican missionaries, their final destination would be the

College of San Fernando de México, a preparatory school for missionaries who would convert the Native Americans. Every ten or fifteen years, the school sent word to Spain that it needed more missionaries. This time, a total of thirty-three were needed, and Fathers Serra and Palóu might be among them. They knew that the difficult trip would take about four to six weeks.

On Easter Sunday, April 6, 1747, Father Serra preached before his parents for the last time. The service was held in San Pedro, the church in which he had been baptized. It was the last time that he would ever see his family.

CHAPTER THREE

A LONG AND DANGEROUS TRIP

Before Fathers Serra and Palóu could begin their journey, they had much to do. They resigned from the university and packed their few things. They told their friends good-bye and went to the Palma harbor. There, they took an English cargo ship that was bound for Málaga, Spain. In Málaga, they would take a ship to Cádiz. The Cádiz ship would take them from Spain to the Americas.

Father Serra realized that he would probably never again see his parents. His father, Antonio Serra, was seventy-three and his mother, Margarita Serra, was seventy-one. Telling them good-bye in person would be too heartbreaking. Instead, he wrote them a letter that he sent from Cádiz. In the letter he wrote, "Always encourage me to go forward, and never to turn back."[1] This saying became his favorite phrase. He also told his family:

> Realize that in order to become a good religious [person]. I have set on this course. So do not be disconsolate. Good-bye, my dear father! Good-bye, dear mother of mine! Good-bye dear sister, Juana! Good-bye, my beloved brother-in-law. Take care of little Mike [his nephew who was about eight and a half years old] and see to it that he becomes a good Christian and a studious pupil and that the two girls [his nieces] grow as good Christians. Trust to God that your uncle may yet be of some service to you. Good-bye and farewell.[2]

The trip from Palma to Málaga, which took fifteen days, began on April 13, 1749. It was the first time that Father Serra and Father Palóu had ever sailed on the open sea. It should have been an enjoyable time, but there were major conflicts with the freighter captain, an Englishman who hated Spanish priests. The captain, with the Bible in his hand, started telling the fathers that Roman Catholicism was wrong and that his faith, Protestantism, was right. Father Serra tried to counter the captain's remarks, but it only made the captain angry. Some nights the captain was furious. Father Palóu wrote that the captain had tried to prevent them from praying, and that once, in a rage, he had threatened to throw them into the sea. The captain also insisted that he was going straight to London without stopping at Málaga. Father Serra answered the captain's threats with a threat of his own: He would report the captain's actions to the king of Spain.[3]

Father Palóu stopped the argument, but it continued the next night. Again, Father Serra argued with the captain. Finally, the captain grabbed him by the throat and screamed, "petty monk of Satan! Recant, or I'll strangle you and throw you to the fishes!"[4] Father Serra fainted, and the captain left. After Father Serra woke up, he returned to his cabin and told Father Palóu what had happened. They stayed awake the entire night, prepared for anything that might happen. They were afraid that the captain might come into their cabin, grab them, and throw them overboard. However, nothing more happened, and they reached Málaga without more problems.

After a five-day wait at Cádiz, where they stayed in the Franciscan convent, they were joined by others who were going to be Mexican missionaries. Most of them were younger than Father Serra. In fact, their average age was twenty-seven.[5]

The Cádiz Board of Trade wrote down the names of all missionaries who left the port. They wrote that Father Serra was a lector (a professor) "native of

Petra, Mallorca; of medium height, swarthy, dark eyes and hair, scant beard."[6]

Cádiz was one of the busiest ports in Europe. From there, ships traveled back and forth to the New World. For hundreds of years, people such as soldiers, adventurers, colonists, and missionaries had left from its harbor to start a new life in the Americas. For the past two hundred years, gold, silver, and spices had been brought to Cádiz from the Indies and the Americas.

In the Franciscan convent, the official who was in charge of finding missionaries for the New World was happy to see Fathers Serra and Palóu. He treated them and the other future missionaries well, but some of the group had second thoughts about going. Five fathers who had never before seen the sea changed their minds. They decided not to travel to Mexico; they were too afraid. Convinced that on the ocean trip there would be monsters, storms, and terrible problems, they returned to their convents.

After these five left, other priests were needed to take their places. Father Serra said that he could secure more missionaries. He suggested that Father Crespí and two other Palma priests be added to the group. These priests were accepted, and they were sent for. The new group arrived in time to sail at the end of August.

Before he left, Father Serra received a letter from a relative who wrote that Father Serra's parents were upset that he was leaving. Father Serra wrote a letter describing his feelings. He sent this farewell letter to his father's cousin, a Petra priest:

> My dear, dear friend, . . . I know that my parents are in mortal grief; . . . it is you upon whom I rely for their comfort . . . Oh, if it were only possible for me to make them share my . . . happiness, they themselves would urge me on! Could they dream, indeed, of a nobler vocation for their son that of a . . . missionary? . . . I recall the promise I made (many years ago) . . . to be a good son of St. Francis . . . to carry out . . . the will of God . . . (to do that) I am on the way to Mexico . . .[7]

On August 28, 1749, Fathers Serra and Palóu were in the first group of missionaries to start the trip from Cádiz to Veracruz, Mexico. From the port of Veracruz, they would travel inland to Mexico City. The ocean voyage to Mexico would take more than three months.

Once they saw the ship, they were uneasy. The ship was in poor condition; it did not look like it could handle the fierce Atlantic storms that could sink better ships. Father Palóu wrote, "On the long voyage of ninety-nine days . . . many inconveniences and scares befell us."[8]

There were too many people packed onto the ship, and there was not enough food and water. Father Serra wrote, "There were moments when my throat was burning so, I would have drunk slime."[9] He never complained, however, and according to Father

Palóu, no one knew that he suffered at all. To deal with it, he told Father Palóu, "the best way of saving one's saliva is to eat little and talk still less."[10]

In spite of the problems, they crossed the ocean safely and reached the island of Puerto Rico. They stayed there for about two weeks, while the boat was resupplied with food and water.

In Puerto Rico, they were guests of a religious group, the Servants of Mary. Although Father Serra and the other fathers had no money at all, he wrote that the people on the island were kind and that they gave the priests chocolate, lemonade, tobacco, and snuff. Father Serra wrote that the missionaries "ate and drank better than in any monastery."[11] This must have seemed like a tremendous luxury after the ship's lack of food and water.

During the Puerto Rico stop, Father Serra held mass and preached to many people. He wrote that "when I preached not a sigh was heard, although I preached a fervent subject and in a loud voice."[12]

They left Puerto Rico for Veracruz on November 1. More troubles were in store for them. Before they could clear the harbor, the wind drove the ship onto the reefs, and it almost sank. After a short delay, they again set sail, but a couple of days before they reached the port of Veracruz, a huge storm hit. Although it was late in the year, it was probably a hurricane. Hurricanes usually occur between June and the end of

October. There can be November hurricanes, but they are less common. The *Villasota* was driven back toward the open sea. The crew was terrified; they were sure they would drown. The storm finally stopped, and they safely anchored in the harbor. After leaving the ship at Veracruz, the missionaries still had a long and hard land trip across a mountainous area of almost two hundred sixty miles to Mexico City.

The *viceroy* (the king's representative in Mexico) had sent a mule-train for them, but it had not yet arrived. Father Serra wanted to get to Mexico City as soon as possible, so he asked his superior if he and a companion could walk. The superior granted his permission. Father Palóu, who was sick, had to stay in Veracruz until he felt better.[13]

Father Serra and the other priest started out on foot, carrying only their religious books. Although they had almost no food or water with them, they felt that God would take care of them. Between December 15, 1749, and January 1, 1750, the two missionaries walked between fifteen and twenty miles a day. Along the way, many people helped them. Once, a stranger appeared and showed them the way across a river. When they ran out of food and water, someone would appear with the needed supplies.

During this part of the trip, Father Serra began having a serious problem that affected him the rest of his life. It started with a bite from one of the many

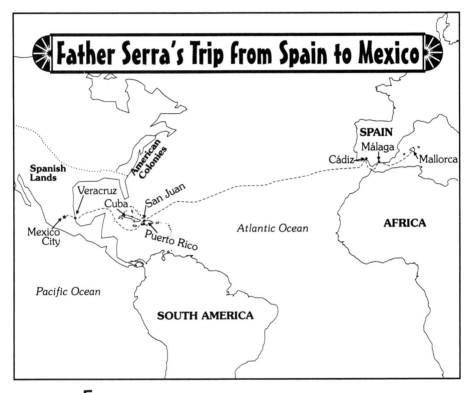

Father Serra's Trip from Spain to Mexico

SPAIN
Málaga
Cádiz
Mallorca

Spanish
Lands

American
Colonies

Veracruz
Cuba
San Juan

Mexico
City

Puerto Rico

Atlantic Ocean

AFRICA

Pacific Ocean

SOUTH AMERICA

Father Serra traveled from Spain to Mexico in 1749.

mosquitoes in the area. Father Serra's badly swollen left foot became infected, and at times the pain was so bad that he could hardly walk. On later trips it would get much worse.

On New Year's Day, Father Serra, hobbling on his painful foot, reached Mexico City and the College of San Fernando. The entire trip from Palma to Mexico City, more than six thousand miles, had taken a long time, but now his new work as a missionary would start. For the next seventeen years, Father Serra's missionary work was based on the directions that he was given by his College of San Fernando superiors.

FATHER SERRA'S WORK IN MEXICO AND BAJA CALIFORNIA

At the time when Father Serra reached the College of San Fernando, Mexico City was the largest North American Spanish city. It was the capital of New Spain and had about one hundred thousand people. The college was located on the city's western side.[1]

When Father Serra arrived, he was warmly greeted by his superior, assigned his new duties, and given a small bedroom. He looked forward to his missionary training; he hoped that he would be able to start right away. The college taught the new missionaries important subjects, especially information that they needed to work with the Native Americans successfully. The college teachers gave them lessons in Native American languages, and they taught the fathers the best ways to instruct the Native Americans about the Roman Catholic religion. The college officials thought that it was important for the missionaries to live with the people whom they hoped to convert. They taught the missionaries the best ways to deal with problems that they would have.[2]

Although he was supposed to complete one full year of training, before the time was up Father Serra volunteered to serve in a mission. The college needed new friars to work in the rugged Sierra Gorda Mountain area; Father Serra volunteered for the work. He was sent to the Sierra Gorda with Father Palóu, who would act as his assistant.[3] The college had started a Sierra Gorda mission about one hundred twenty miles north of Mexico City. The mission was to serve as a center to convert the Pame people who lived in the area. For the few Spaniards in the area, the mission was a center to strengthen their religious training and maintain their Spanish culture.

The Pames were hunters and gatherers; they also grew some crops. For many years, they had fought against Spanish control by hiding in the mountains and attacking Spanish soldiers from their base. They raided and burned Spanish farms, and they also robbed travelers.

The Spanish did not understand the Pame language and culture. One author wrote that it was difficult to civilize the Pames. He considered them "dirty, boisterous, lazy, . . . drunkards; in the habit of lying, cheating, stealing, killing people, who begged without shame and enjoyed the sight of suffering."[4]

Serra left for this tough assignment about six months after he reached Mexico. Spanish soldiers and converted Native Americans leading pack animals went with Father Serra into the mountains. Father Serra again decided to walk. In terrible heat, the trip took them sixteen days. The travelers also suffered from mosquitoes, fleas, and chiggers. The region had deer, coyotes, poisonous snakes, and beautiful birds, including parrots. For Father Serra, the trip was especially difficult because his leg swelled up.

They finally reached the little village of Jalpán. Although it had a small adobe mission and church, Father Serra found that the natives had learned little about the Roman Catholic religion.[5] Fathers Serra and Palóu would have to work hard to convert the Pames. Father Palóu wrote:

> Seeing these missions in so backward a state . . . [Father Serra] applied himself . . . to learning their language. For this purpose he had as teacher an Indian from Mexico City who had

been reared among the Pames. . . . Thus he began to pray with the Indians in their native tongue, every other day . . . [using] the catechism [prayers] in Spanish.[6]

Father Serra realized that the Pames could not understand religious theory, so he would have to teach them in a different way. He decided to interest them through drama and stories. Every Saturday night, he held a parade through the town in which one person carried a statue of Mary. He helped the Pame children organize a Christmas play. Although he said that he knew little about music, he used songs and hymns to interest the Pames. He also taught them to stage other religious plays.[7]

Father Serra knew that it was also important to make certain that the mission could support the Pames who lived there, as well as teach them Spanish customs. He had the College of San Fernando send cattle, goats, sheep, and farming tools to the mission. With the other fathers, he taught the Pame men how to grow crops such as cabbage, melon, lettuce, and beans. They also taught the Pames Spanish cooking. They taught the women to spin thread, sew, knit, and make wicker trays and baskets. The extra goods that the mission Pames did not need were sold at nearby market towns. The Pames who learned quickly were rewarded. They were assigned land of their own on which they grew corn, beans, and pumpkins.

The fathers were more successful than they had hoped to be. The Pame people gave up many of their old ways and became successful villagers and farmers. Because of Father Serra's work on his parents' farm in Mallorca, he knew many farming skills, which he taught to the Pames.

Within a few years, Father Serra, using Pame labor, started building a new, larger stone church. He often worked on it alongside the Pames; seven years later, it was finished. It is still standing and is used for church services today. For eight years, Father Serra lived in the Sierra Gordas. During this time, other missionaries built more churches under his supervision.

Most of his plans were carried out, but the Spanish military leader who had conquered the Pames in 1743 allowed Spanish soldiers and their families to settle on Pame land. He did this to establish Spanish life in the area and to reward the Spanish soldiers who had served the king. As a result, there were many conflicts with the Pames. The soldiers had been promised land, but there was little land available that was good for farming. Acting on behalf of the Pames, the missions also claimed the land. The missions needed the land to grow the food needed for the mission Pames. Finally, the viceroy became involved.

The major conflict started when some of the soldiers' families were told by the Sierra Gorda military leader that they could have any land that they wanted. Spanish law said otherwise. The Law of the Indies, the Spanish law that was used in the Spanish colonies, forbade settlements in territories that were mission-held. Meanwhile, the Pames said that they would use force, if necessary, to defend their land. The College of San Fernando and Father Serra supported the Pames.[8]

When the viceroy was told about the conflict, he ruled that the missions were right, that the soldiers and their families who had started a town must leave. The soldiers refused, and there were not enough loyal soldiers to force them out. Finally, after a long legal fight, the soldier settlers left.[9] In 1755, the fathers and the Pames regained the land.[10]

At this time, Father Serra almost became a Texas missionary. In a Native American attack, several Franciscan fathers at the San Saba mission, in what is today central Texas, were killed. His superior sent word to the Sierra Gorda that Father Serra should return to Mexico City. From there, he would take over the dead fathers' Texas work.

When Father Serra reached Mexico City, he was jolted by the noisy crowds and traffic. He had become used to the quiet, lonely Sierra Gorda that he had come to know so well. While he was at the college, he learned more about the San Saba mission attack. Father Molina, the only missionary to survive the

Native American attack, returned to the college to recover from his arm wound. The Native Americans had killed two other missionaries who had been there with him.[11]

The San Saba mission was started in 1757; a presidio was built two miles away. No Native Americans lived nearby. From time to time, Apaches and other Native American tribes traveled through the area and camped near the mission. When the presidio commander found out that the Native Americans were hostile, he asked for permission to close the mission; there were too few soldiers to defend it. The viceroy refused.

Shortly after that, a major Native American attack took place. One morning, about two thousand Native Americans appeared armed with bows and arrows, as well as with guns that had been sold to them by the French in Louisiana.[12] Most of the Native Americans were Comanches; some were Apaches. The Native Americans attacked and burned the mission. One priest was killed; others were injured. Father Molina lived because he had found a hiding place. He was, however, wounded by an arrow. At night, they reached the safety of the presidio.[13]

The Spanish government decided to put down the Native American revolt. At first, the Spanish troops were successful, then came defeats. In the meantime,

the Mexican viceroy had died. The new viceroy
thought that Spain first should take care of more
important matters.[14] Father Serra's order to leave
for Texas was canceled.

Father Serra may have been disappointed that
he was not going, but as always, he obeyed. He
spent the next nine years at the College of San
Fernando as a home missionary. He traveled as a
preacher through various areas of Mexico. Each
year, he spent about four months at the college and
eight months on his preaching tours. During these
years, he traveled over five thousand miles.[15]

During these years at the college, he often gave
sermons in Mexico City that caused people to be
angry with him. Many wealthy Spanish women
attended church, not to pray but instead to visit with
their friends. During services, some of the women
would have their servants bring them chocolate to
drink. Father Serra spoke out against these practices,
but all it did was make the women angry.[16]

He made worse enemies. Once he was told that
the wine used for services had been poisoned, but he
ignored the warning. He drank, and then "he visibly
changed color and was rendered partly speechless.
Nevertheless, he took [more, but] he lost his speech
altogether."[17] He almost passed out and was carried
into a room and placed on the bed. One witness said
that someone had tried to kill him.[18]

While he was at the college, Father Serra worked with his usual dedication. To fit in as much work as he could, he trained himself to need little sleep. Often, he would sleep from 8:00 P.M. until midnight and then pray until morning. He also ate very little. He rarely ate meat and had only small amounts of fruit, fish, and vegetables.

Father Serra was highly regarded as a preacher. In a 1767 trip to a remote area, he paddled up a difficult river. The heat, flies, and alligators made conditions dangerous. In fact, because of the wild animals and

This is Father Serra's room at Mission San Carlos Borromeo de Carmelo. He slept on a bed of boards covered by one blanket.

poisonous snakes, Father Serra and his companions could not get out of the canoes for one week. When they could leave the canoes, they had to walk many miles over the rugged mountain land. Even though he was exhausted from the trip, during his four months in the area, Father Serra preached many times.

In one small town, Father Serra held services, but few people were there. After he left, an epidemic swept the town, taking sixty lives. The local priest remarked that only those who had been in Father Serra's services were spared. There is no way to know if this is what really happened, but after hearing this story, people started flocking to Father Serra's sermons.

Father Serra did not know that his Mexican work would soon end. Events taking place in Europe and North America would lead him to California.

An order issued by the Spanish king changed Father Serra's life. In 1767, King Carlos III expelled the Jesuits, an order of priests, from *Baja* (Lower) California. The Jesuits had done missionary work throughout the world. No one knows for certain why King Carlos expelled them from California, but one theory is that he thought that the Spanish Jesuits had too much political power.

The king sent the order to the viceroy in Mexico City. He told the viceroy to appoint a leader to "Repair with an armed force to the houses of Jesuits. Seize the persons . . . and within twenty-four hours transport them as prisoners to the port of Veracruz."[18]

The Jesuits were soon gone, and the College of San Fernando was told to supply Baja California with new missionaries. The college leaders met, and they picked Father Serra to be the superior in charge of the Baja Franciscan missions. In July 1767, Father Serra and the other missionaries picked for this job left Mexico and began their journey north.

After a long trip over land and sea, they reached their goal: Loreto, the Baja California capital. From there, Father Serra would send missionaries to the fifteen Baja missions. When they arrived in Loreto, the fathers found poor conditions. There were only about seven thousand Christians in the entire area and some of them had not really learned Spanish customs. "[M]any . . . were still running around nude."[19] The region had little food, and the semidesert Baja was almost barren.

Father Serra's headquarters was at the Loreto mission. The governor, Gaspar de Portolá, with his officers, welcomed the group. He gave Father Serra control of the Loreto church. In addition to the church, the governor gave the fathers food as well as rooms to be used as bedrooms and offices.

Although Father Serra was able to control religious matters, he learned that the governor expected to be in charge of the missions. Father Serra had no choice but to agree.

For one year, Father Serra stayed at the Loreto mission, directing the fathers' work. It was a very difficult job. To help attract Native Americans to the missions, they had to provide a stable food source but it was hard to grow crops because there was so little water. Also, there were fewer Native Americans than when the Spanish first had taken control of the Baja. The Spanish soldiers had exposed the Native Americans to new diseases, including syphilis and measles. Because the Native Americans had no immunity to the Spanish diseases, many died.

While Serra and his group were struggling in Baja, another event, this time in *Alta* (Upper) California, changed his life. For many reasons, the Spanish government decided to claim Alta California formally in the king's name. To achieve that goal and to make certain that the region would be stable, they decided it was time to start missions there. This plan totally changed Father Serra's life. Finally, he would reach his lifelong dream: to work in a place where no missionary had been before.

SPAIN AND CALIFORNIA

Spain's interest in California began at least two hundred years before Father Serra reached California. After Spain was unified by King Ferdinand and Queen Isabella in the late 1400s, it grew rich and powerful. In the fifteenth and sixteenth centuries, Spain started colonies throughout the New World. The Spanish goals were God, gold, and glory.

Spain used appointed officials to govern the colonies. The king and his advisors appointed a viceroy to govern for a one-year period. The viceroy then selected other men for many jobs. The viceroy of New Spain was in charge of the California missions as well as all exploring and colonizing efforts. The viceroy of New Spain lived in the capital, Mexico City.

Spain had long been interested in California. The first Spanish explorer in the area was Hernando Cortés. In Mexico, Cortés had conquered the Aztec nation. Always looking for more gold, he explored Baja California but found it a poor land. Cortés, and other explorers who followed him, searched for gold in California. They may have thought that California was a land of gold because they had heard or read the Spanish story about the strange Queen Califia and her group of Amazons.

Queen Califia was mentioned in a Spanish romantic novel, *Las Sergas de Esplandián* (The Exploits of Esplandian). The story was about an attack on Christians who lived in the Turkish capital Constantinople. During the battle, Queen Califia helped the attacking forces. She was described as a warrior queen who came from a place:

> . . . at the right hand of the Indies, an island named California, very close to that part . . . which is inhabited by black women, without a single man among them, who live in the manner of Amazons. . . . Their weapons were made of gold. The island everywhere abounds with [contains] gold and precious stones and upon it no other metal is found.[1]

Although Cortés had no luck in finding gold, people continued to use the name Califia to describe

California. For many years, California was thought to be an island. In 1705, a map was drawn that fixed the mistake. The new map finally showed the Baja as a peninsula attached to the mainland, Alta California.

Because little was known about the region, there were several Spanish efforts to explore Alta California. The Spanish wanted to find good harbors along the coast for their ships. They also were looking for places to start colonies. Two sea expeditions, in 1542 and 1602, only sailed up the coast, stopped briefly, and recorded information about the land.

One effort to explore California actually came from an Englishman, Sir Francis Drake. On his way home from a successful raid on Spanish treasure ships, he landed his damaged ship north of what is now San Francisco. There, he made the needed repairs. He was pleased with the land that he saw. Claiming it for England's Queen Elizabeth I, he named it New Albion (Albion was an old name for England). After Drake returned to England, the government sent an English group to colonize California, but it never arrived. The Spanish attacked and destroyed the English fleet off the Brazilian coast, and England lost interest in the area.

Explorers working for the Spanish crown continued to sail along the California coast. In 1542, Juan Rodríguez Cabrillo, who was Portuguese-born, made a chart of the coast. The Spanish government had ordered him to search for a northwest passage to

45

the Atlantic Ocean. On September 28, 1542, he entered what is now called San Diego Bay. He named the area San Miguel, in honor of the feast of San Miguel (St. Michael), which took place on that day.[2]

In 1602, the explorer Sebastián Vizcaíno left a small port on Mexico's western side and followed Cabrillo's route. With four well-stocked ships, he explored the California coast. When he first saw the Baja, it looked so much like a desert that he gave parts of it such names as Hills of Horror and Cape Desert. When he reached Alta California, the scenery changed. The semidesert Baja landscape was replaced by one that was lush and green.

He also named and renamed many Alta sites. He renamed San Miguel, San Diego, because he reached it on San Diego's (St. Didacus's) feast day. In the north, he sighted a beautiful bay and named it Monterey, after the Mexican viceroy. In the name of Spain, he also claimed many other important coastal locations. He thought the area was so beautiful that he called it a Garden of Eden. He found the Native Americans to be handsome and friendly. He decided that instead of the Spanish settling in the Baja, they should settle in Alta California.[3]

After Vizcaino's sea voyage, more than one hundred years passed before the Spanish again became interested in California. By then, Spain's empire and control had grown. Spain owned New World lands from the tip of South America through Texas and Florida.

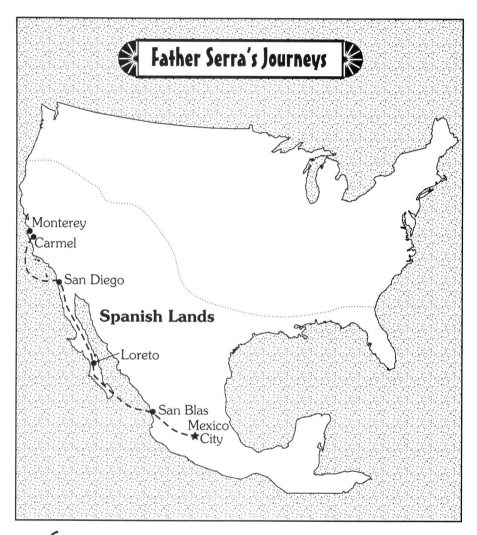

Father Serra's Journeys

Monterey
Carmel
San Diego

Spanish Lands

Loreto

San Blas
Mexico
City

Spanish explorers first traveled to California in search of gold. Other countries began to send explorers for gold and to form colonies. Later, Father Serra traveled to Baja and Alta California.

There were missions in Mexico and in Baja California. However, Spain showed no interest in the upper Pacific coast area until other countries expressed interest in the region. Russia, England, France, and Prussia started to plan explorations. The Spanish were afraid that this would lead to one or more of these countries claiming the land.

Russia, especially, was a threat to Spanish interests in California. The Russians had started to move south from Alaska, their North American colony. To protect their claims, they built a fort in northern California. When King Carlos III of Spain heard about Russia's movement into what Spain claimed as Spanish land, he decided that something had to be done. It would be impossible for Spain to keep its one-thousand-mile Mexican frontier if the Russians gained control of California and its surrounding areas. One Spanish official said of Russia's threat, "This stirring nation spares no money, diligence, or fatigue in advancing her discoveries."[4]

To meet the Russian threat, Carlos III decided to send more missionaries and settlers to Alta California. The Spanish government picked two California sites for missions: San Diego in the South, and Monterey in the North.

Neither the king, government, military, nor the missionaries cared about the wishes of the Native Americans. The Spanish saw the conversion of Native Americans to Catholicism as doing God's work.

In 1769, when the Spanish government first moved into California, there were about three hundred thousand native people. With a moderate climate and a good, stable food supply, the California coastal area had more Native Americans per square mile than any other part of what is now the United States. Among the Native Americans, there were more than a hundred large cultural groups; each had its own identity, territory, and customs. There were more than a hundred languages spoken. Most of the languages were so different from each other that tribes were unable to understand each other.[5]

The Native Americans' way of life was very different from that of the Spanish, especially in clothing and personal decoration, food, and work. In many coastal tribes, the Native American men wore little or no clothing; the women often wore deerskin skirts. They decorated their bodies with brightly painted designs and tattoos.[6]

For food, the Native Americans used what nature provided. They mainly hunted and fished; most of the tribes did not plant crops or herd flocks. In the coastal areas they made fishing boats. The men hunted with bows and arrows and trapped game. They killed dear, rabbit, bear, mice, and birds. The women gathered seeds, nuts, and fruits. Native people also ate other food, including grasshoppers, lizards, snakes, and worms.

49

Some people grew tobacco that was used in religious rituals. They kept dogs for hunting and for companionship, but most of the tribes did not raise animals as a food source.[7]

Considering how much the Native Americans had to eat, it is strange that the Spanish had survival problems. The Spanish thought that the Native Americans were savages, yet it was the Spanish who almost died from lack of food after they first settled the area. For a long time, the Spanish had to rely on food brought into the country by ships. When the ships did not arrive, they starved. When it arrived, the food was often spoiled.

Unlike the Spanish, the Native Americans had no written language. Before the Spanish came, they were healthy. In one Spanish Alta California mission, the fathers found few signs of health problems among the first 4,771 adult Native Americans who were baptized. Out of the almost five thousand Native Americans that they saw, only thirty were sick. The Native Americans' sicknesses included blindness, lameness, or mental illness. The Native Americans' health needs were taken care of by a medicine man and by home remedies made from roots, herbs, and berries.[8] Their remedies were usually successful.

Another difference from the Spanish was in housing. Many California coastal Native Americans lived in cone-shaped homes made of brush, in villages near water or oak groves. When their homes became too dirty, they burned them and built new ones.[9]

Their weapons and tools were made of stone, wood, and bone. They wove baskets so tightly that they could be used to carry water. The Native Americans who lived near the Santa Barbara area built such well-made plank boats that they are considered to be among the finest boats ever built by Native Americans in what is now the United States. The boats could be rowed very quickly and were very fast. Each could carry between ten and twelve people.[10]

Like many other Native Americans, most California tribes used the *temescal* (sweat house). The temescal, used only by men, was like a sauna. The heat from a big fire built in the center caused them to sweat. The men would sit in front of the fire and then run outside and plunge into the water. It was considered a good way to stay healthy.[11]

The men hunted and fished, and made weapons and tools. The women gathered plants, seeds, and nuts; they also cooked and took care of the children.[12]

Rules about owning property were based on each tribe's customs. Tribal village members jointly used lands, mines, and quarries. Other property, such as oak groves, grass fields, hunting areas, and fishing sites, sometimes were used by families. The Native Americans were more concerned with claims by other tribes than they were with individually-owned property within their own tribe.[13]

Marriage was difficult because a young person had to look for a marriage partner in another village. The young men and women had a great deal of choice in picking their mates, but parents and other relatives played an important role.[14]

The groom's family was expected to give the bride's family bridal gifts. The gifts could be shellbeads, animal skin blankets, and food. In central California, the bride's family also had to give gifts to the groom's family. The bride's family's gifts were often less valuable than those given by the groom. In other areas, the gift exchange favored the groom's family.[15]

Most Native American men had one wife, but rich men often had two or three. It was common for the wives to be sisters, since this meant that they usually would get along well together.[16]

In many tribes, both women and men were able to divorce. A man could divorce a woman if she could not have children or if she was lazy. A woman could divorce a man if he beat her or was cruel to her. How easy or hard it was to divorce was based on the bridal gifts that the married couple had been given. In groups where bridal gifts were very important, divorces were less common because the bride or groom would have to give the gifts back. When a divorce took place, the woman and children would return to the woman's home village.[17]

The missionaries had problems understanding and dealing with these customs. They found it very difficult to work with a Native American culture that was based on personal freedom and individuality. This caused great conflicts between the fathers and the Native Americans. The fathers, who wanted the Native Americans to adopt a Spanish lifestyle, felt that they had the right to make them give up their customs and become part of a highly organized group mission life. One estimate is that during the mission period, one hundred thousand of the three hundred thousand California Native Americans became Roman Catholics.[18]

The Spanish king told the viceroy that it was time for the Spanish to settle in California. To start the settlement program, people were selected to plan and carry it out. The viceroy and the College of San Fernando selected people for these jobs. Father Serra was given orders to start the Alta California missions and to convert the Native Americans who lived there. He was made mission president, which meant that he would be in charge of all the missions that were built.

The viceroy selected people to head the Alta expedition. The Spanish inspector-general, José de Gálvez, was placed in charge. Gálvez, in turn, selected Captain Gaspar de Portolá to be the military chief of the land and sea groups that would be sent. (Portolá was later appointed the first California governor.)

The government planned to use the missions to make colonizing California easier. If Father Serra and the other fathers had good relations with the Native Americans, this would prevent attacks that would delay the government's work. Once Serra had built the missions and convinced the Native Americans to live on their grounds, the Spanish government could consider starting Spanish towns. To keep the Native Americans at the missions, the fathers would teach them the Roman Catholic faith as well as European farming skills.

To develop a stable mission food source, farming was vital. In time, the missions would be able to feed everyone who lived in them. Once the missions could support themselves and the Native Americans were peaceful, Spanish settlers would be allowed to move into nearby areas.

Father Serra's appointment as mission president meant that his boyhood dream would come true. He would be a missionary in a distant land, and more important, he would go where no other missionaries had gone before.

José de Gálvez started to make plans for the Alta trips. He discussed the plans with Father Serra and strongly considered his advice.

TWO MISSIONS ARE BUILT

 In working out the plans to start the Alta missions, Gálvez and Father Serra agreed on many important issues. They decided that a chain of coastal missions should be built and that the missions should be one day's trip apart. The first mission would be San Diego, in the South; the second would be Monterey, in the North, almost five hundred miles away. A third mission was planned for what is today the Santa Barbara Channel. Other missions would be built between San Diego and Monterey until they reached the goal of ten. If only the first three could be built, then two missionaries would be placed at each. To

This replica of a wooden cross is at Mission Santa Bárbara. The mission was founded in 1786.

ensure the safety of the three missions, Gálvez would station soldiers between them. The soldiers would remain in place until more missions could be built.

They also discussed other issues such as the money to fund the missions and the names that would be picked for them. The funds to start the missions would be provided by the money that was taken from the Baja Jesuits who had been forced to leave. The missions would have religious names. Father Serra wanted them named for Franciscan saints. He especially wanted one that would be named for St. Francis of Assisi; Gálvez agreed.[1]

Father Serra was anxious to start the California trip, but before he could leave, he experienced terrible pain from his foot and leg infections. Because the swelling almost crippled him, the military leader of the expedition, Gaspar de Portolá, asked Father Serra to stay behind and send someone in his place. Portolá was afraid that Father Serra would not survive the long trip. Father Palóu also was concerned about Father Serra's health; he offered to go in his place. Father Serra refused; he said that God would guide his trip to both places, San Diego and Monterey.[2]

When Father Palóu learned that Father Serra had set his mind on going, he wrote, "When I saw him and his swollen foot and leg . . . I could not keep back the tears when I thought of how much he . . . had to suffer in the rough and dessert trails."[3]

Meanwhile, Gálvez worked out the trip details: There would be four groups starting from various locations in Baja California that would travel to Alta California. The expeditions would leave from Santa María, and the two sea expeditions would leave from La Paz. Each group would start out at a different time and they would meet at the site of the first planned mission, San Diego. From there, at least one or more groups would travel to Monterey and start the northern mission.[4]

The sea expeditions would have two ships, the *San Carlos* and the *San Antonio*. The *San Carlos* would sail on January 9, 1769, a month before the second ship. The ships would carry soldiers and crew, building materials, and important foods such as oil, dates, wine, vinegar, and brandy. Each land group would leave at the same time as a ship. One group would be led by Captain Fernando de Rivera, and the other would be led by Portolá.

They thought that the ships would take about four months to reach San Diego and that the land groups would make the trip in half that time. If the land groups could cover twelve and a half miles each day, they could travel the three hundred twenty-five miles in two months or less. The land groups would also take with them supplies and cattle.

Father Serra selected the missionaries for the trips. Father Crespí, his former student from Palma, would go with Rivera. Father Serra would travel with Portolá. The other four missionaries would sail on the ships.

Although Father Serra's foot and leg problems had not improved, he managed to travel hundreds of miles, visiting the Baja missions and getting things ready for the trip. By now, the swelling covered more than half of his left leg.

Finally, the work was finished. The *San Carlos* sailed in January 1769, the *San Antonio* in February. At the end of March, Father Serra started his own trip; he wanted to join Portolá's group and travel with it to San Diego.

Rivera had already left with his group several weeks earlier. The twenty-nine soldiers with him wore sleeveless leather jackets that served as armor in case of a Native American attack. They also had forty-two converted Baja Native Americans with them. On May 14, when Rivera and his group reached San Diego, they found two ships already there.

When Father Serra joined Portolá, the pain in his leg was so bad that he asked one of the men who took care of the mules to give him the same medicine that he used on lame mules. The mule-tender's cure, herbs mixed with wax, worked—the leg was less painful. Father Serra could again ride the old mule that he had been given.

The expedition left from Loreto, almost nine hundred miles south of San Diego. It followed the other land group's route. During the trip, Father Serra was pleased at his chance to convert Native Americans. When he first saw them he wrote, "I could hardly believe . . . that they go about entirely naked . . . although they saw all of us clothed, they nevertheless showed not the least trace of shame."[5]

Father Serra's first impression of the California Native Americans was, "Their grace, vigor, friendliness, and gaiety are charming."[6]

As a sign of friendship, Father Serra placed his hands on the Native Americans' heads and blessed them. He also gave them figs which they liked. The Native Americans, in return, gave him and the others fish. Father Serra decided to start a mission at the place where they met the Native Americans. The place was named Velicatá.

The group with Father Serra was made up of twenty-five soldiers, thirty converted Native Americans, cooks, laborers, and interpreters. With them, they had about one hundred cows and one hundred seventy mules and donkeys. The white men had swords and guns; the Native Americans were allowed to have only bows and arrows. Portolá and Father Serra rode in the front.[7]

Slowly, they covered the miles, stopping often to rest. They followed the coast, but at times they had to change their route to find water and grass. Sometimes, they had to search for ways to cross the mountains or to find ways around them. Father Serra often gave saints' names to places that he passed.

At the end of May, more Native Americans were seen following the travelers. The soldiers captured one of them, tied him up, and brought him to the camp. The young man was very upset because of the way he had been treated, but after they gave him food, he felt better. He told Portolá that he was sorry that he was spying. He also said that his tribe was going to ambush the Spaniards. Serra and the other group leaders decided to forgive him and send him back to his people. After he reached his tribe, he told them how well he had been treated, and they called off their attack.

Although Father Serra and his companions were relieved that the Native Americans were friendly, other things made their lives miserable. Fleas and ticks bit them. They had plenty of water one day, but none, or poor quality water, the next. Serra wrote: "Half walking . . . stumbling and scrambling to our feet only to fall again, we made our toilsome way into the valley."[8] Conditions were so bad that nine converted Native Americans quietly left the group.

On June 23, they spotted a large group of Native Americans. Father Serra described them as "healthy and well built, affable and . . . happy." The Spanish thought that they were very smart because they could quickly repeat all the Spanish words that they heard. They also danced, offered the Spanish fish and mussels, and asked them to stay. Father Serra wrote, "We were all enamored [with] . . . them. . . . In fact all the pagans have pleased me, but these . . . have stolen my heart."[9]

The Native Americans' dress and decoration were very different from what the Spanish wore. The men were naked; the women wore some clothing. Their hair was plastered with white clay. They wore hair crowns made of beaver skin or fur. They liked trading with the soldiers.[10]

As the group neared San Diego, more and more Native Americans followed them. The Spanish thought that they were rude. If Father Serra put his hands on their heads, they did the same to him. If he sat down, they sat down right next to him. The Native Americans also were curious about Spanish things; one man almost got away with Father Serra's glasses.[11]

As they traveled north, the land became greener and more beautiful. There were lovely flowers, including poppies and roses, as well as grape vines. One of the flowers that Father Serra admired, later known as Rosa California, grew along the entire California coast.[12]

Finally, in late June 1769, they reached San Diego Bay. As they traveled along the shoreline, they could see the bay and the two Spanish ships that had reached San Diego before them. They were tired but hopeful.

On July 1, 1769, Portolá's and Rivera's groups were reunited. Father Serra wrote, "It was a day of great rejoicing and merriment . . . Thanks be to God."[13] Father Serra was pleased that they had reached their goal and that they could start their work. He did not realize how hard it would be to make the missions succeed.

The happiness of Portolá, Father Serra, and the rest of the group quickly changed to horror when Rivera told them what had happened. Many of the men who were needed to start building the missions were dying or dead. Of the 219 who had set out with the land groups, only half were left, and of the half, many were sick. To make matters worse, there were also many deaths among the those who had sailed to San Diego. Most of the ships' crews and more than half of the soldiers had died.[14] Health experts today would blame most of the soldiers' deaths on scurvy.

> Over a long period of time a diet deficient in . . . Vitamin C, which is found in fruit, green vegetables and fresh milk, will cause scurvy. The diet of sailors in those days consisted of biscuits and salt or dried meat. The effects of scurvy are bleeding gums . . . loss of teeth, ulcers of the limbs, anemia and general debility increasing until death.[15]

A water source was needed right away. They asked the local Native Americans for help, but at first they were refused. After they were given gifts of ribbons, glass, beads, and other items, the Native Americans showed the travelers a nearby river.

Meanwhile, Portolá made a number of decisions: He ordered the *San Antonio* to leave on July 9 and return to northern Mexico to bring back more supplies. He also decided that it was time to take one group and travel to Monterey. Portolá, with a group of seventy-five men, left on July 14 to search for Monterey Bay. Fathers Crespí and Gómez traveled with him.

In June, a third ship was sent to San Diego from Mexico, carrying badly needed supplies. The ship ran into storms, and after three months at sea, it returned to Mexico. The following spring, it again left for San Diego, loaded with "ten thousand pounds of dried meat, eight casks of good wine, two casks of brandy, twelve hundred and fifty pounds of dried figs, many bushels of beans, . . . raisins and dried fish. . . a church bell, vestments for the fathers, trading materials for the Native American converts."[16] These goods, which were so badly needed, never arrived.

While they waited for supplies, Father Serra decided it was time to start building the mission. On July 16, 1769, he proudly raised a wooden cross on the first California mission site. On the slope of a hill that overlooked the bay, he held mass and gave a sermon. He named the mission in honor of St. Didacus, known in Spanish as San Diego. He was a

Franciscan who lived in an area of Spain called the Alcalá, in the province of Castile.[17]

As Father Serra raised the cross and started the process that led to the building of the first mission, San Diego de Alcalá, a few Native Americans quietly watched. They did not know that these events and the others that would follow would change their lives forever.

The Native Americans who watched Father Serra looked like those they had seen on the trip. The men and boys were naked; the women and girls wore aprons made of leaves and reeds. The missionaries were unable to talk with the Native Americans because neither the Spaniards nor the Baja Native Americans whom they had brought with them understood the local language. It is estimated that the Native Americans in California spoke at least eighteen major languages.[18]

Father Serra was pleased by the scene that he observed. The group camped on what is now called Presidio Hill. They found the land lush; they would be able to grow many crops and there were trees, game, and fish. This site was on a point that overlooked San Diego Bay, near Cosoy, a Native American village.[19] For these reasons, Presidio Hill became the camp headquarters. They built simple huts and a small church.

The first month was very hard. Relations with the Native Americans got worse, and in August, the mission was attacked. On August 15, Father Parrón,

This sculpture represents the wooden cross that was raised on Presidio Hill. The first mission, San Diego de Alcalá, was built there, but later was moved to another site.

who had stayed at San Diego de Alcalá with Father Serra, went with several soldiers to hold services for the crew of the *San Carlos*. When the Native Americans saw that few people were protecting the mission, twenty men armed with bows and arrows attacked. The few soldiers who were left in the mission ran to get their guns. They were helped by the mission blacksmith and carpenter.

Father Serra stayed inside a hut during the attack. As he was praying that the attack would end, his converted Baja Native American servant burst into the hut. There was an arrow piercing his neck. He said to Father Serra, "Father, absolve me; the Indians have killed me." He died at Father Serra's feet.[20]

By the time the attack ended, many Spaniards had been wounded. Three Native Americans had been killed; several were wounded. Dr. Pedro Prat, who was at the settlement, treated both the Spaniards and the injured Native Americans.[21]

The San Diego battle actually turned the tide of Spanish-Native American relations. The Native Americans were grateful to the doctor who had treated their wounds. They also found out how dangerous Spanish guns were. After that, for a while, the Native Americans were peaceful. Later, there was another, more dangerous attack. To better protect the mission, the soldiers set a circle of wood poles into the ground around it.[22]

Although their relationship with the Native Americans improved, the Spanish still faced starvation. Unlike the Native Americans, they were not able to feed themselves from the land. Also, they did not have the right kind of clothes or shelter. Miguel Costansó, who was among the few surviving *San Carlos* crew, wrote that the soldiers suffered because of the extreme temperatures (cold at night and hot by day). Several soldiers died each day.[23]

In the meantime, Rivera was on his way to Monterey. Father Crespí, who went with him, described the many unusual things they saw. At first, the countryside provided plenty of food. They shot deer and killed bear. They also passed the Los Angeles area, where they felt a slight earthquake. They described and named the "huge trees of reddish-colored wood," the redwood forests. They were probably among the first white men to gaze at San Francisco Bay.[24]

They continued looking for Monterey Bay, but they could not find it. They knew they were in the Monterey area. So, at what they thought was a nearby bay, they decided to raise a cross. On the cross, Father Crespí wrote, "Dig! At the foot thou wilt find a writing."[25] They kept looking for Monterey Bay, but could not find it. They finally gave up their search and decided to return to San Diego.

On January 27, 1770, the seventy-five men reached the southern camp. They were tired and hungry but were glad to be alive. The two groups were glad to see each other, but the San Diego group was surprised to find that the men who had gone north smelled like mules. The Rivera group told them that on the return trip they were unable to find enough food. Rather than starve, they had to eat some of their mules.

The Native Americans that the Portolá group met had been friendly, but Portolá's group had not found Monterey Bay. In fact, Rivera said, there was no such bay. They had found another bay that was big enough to hold European ships, but it was not the bay described by the explorer Vizcaíno.[26]

With more mouths to feed, the conditions at San Diego de Alcalá got worse. They waited without luck for the much-longed-for supply ship, the *San José*, which had been lost at sea. Portolá told Father Serra if a ship did not come by March 19, then they would all return to the Baja. The idea of giving up made Father Serra almost sick.

On March 19, after breakfast, the soldiers packed their few belongings, getting ready for the march south. Then, at about 3:00 P.M., a ship was sighted. Someone yelled out, "Sail!" Everyone cheered; it was the *San Antonio*, a different ship than the one expected, but one carrying plenty of supplies. The mission was saved.[27]

Now that the San Diego mission had supplies, Portolá and Father Serra made new plans. Portolá, with

Father Crespí, would head north with his men. Father Serra would sail on the *San Antonio* and join Portolá at Monterey. Fathers Parrón and Gómez would be left in charge of the San Diego mission. After the Monterey mission had been built, Father Crespí would travel south and start Mission San Buenaventura, somewhere on the Santa Barbara Channel.

They were certain that this time they would find Monterey. In fact, they now thought that it must be the large bay where Portolá's group had raised a cross. They finally decided they had reached Monterey Bay, but had identified it incorrectly. The description that they had carried with them had been of a view from the sea, not from land. Also, the trees and flowers that grew there did not match the description because they had arrived in a different season than the one described by earlier explorers. Once they took these factors into account, they were certain that the bay they had seen was Monterey. They decided to meet at the cross. It turned out that they were right—the bay where they had raised a cross was indeed Monterey.

When Portolá reached Monterey, he found the cross that he had planted the winter before. It was a strange sight—the cross was surrounded by a number of things: meat, shellfish, arrows that had been planted in the ground, and a string of sardines. The Native Americans, knowing that the cross was important to the Spanish, decided to use it as a place to leave offerings for their own gods.

One week after Portolá arrived, the *San Antonio* sailed into Monterey Bay. On June 3, 1770, as the Native Americans watched, Fathers Serra and Crespí said prayers and named the new mission. They called it Mission San Carlos Borromeo (St. Charles of Borromeo) for St. Charles, a church official who lived in the 1500s. After Father Serra gave the sermon, Governor Portolá claimed the land for the Spanish king.

After the ceremonies were over, the group started building a presidio and a mission. Within a month, they were done. A few cannons manned by a small group of soldiers protected the fort. Governor Portolá, his work done, left Lieutenant Pedro Fages in charge. When news that the missions had been started reached Mexico City, there was a big celebration.

Again, they had been successful, but there were many problems. They still did not have enough supplies. They had to deal with a lot of Spanish government red tape. There were conflicts between Father Serra and the military leaders. Also, they had to always be on guard against hostile Native Americans, who, although they seemed friendly, could change and attack them at any time. Father Serra's skills and abilities helped them deal with all these conflicts.

Later, Monterey was named the Alta California capital. It was Father Serra's most loved mission, as

Father Serra used Mission San Carlos de Borromeo de Carmelo as his headquarters. The mission's church is still used for religious services.

well as his headquarters. Although he liked the site on which the church and buildings were located, he wrote in a letter to his superiors that the mission might have to be moved to another area. Indeed, the mission was relocated to Carmel, another lovely spot, and renamed San Carlos Borromeo de Carmelo. There, it was close to a Native American village, there was available drinking water, and it was farther away from the Monterey presidio.

Father Serra wrote to the College of San Fernando asking to be sent more missionaries, especially hardworking ones. He wrote, "Those who come here dedicated to so holy a work must undergo sacrifices. . . . In these distant parts, one must expect to suffer some hardships, but these will be even more burdensome [hard] to those who are seeking . . . comfort."[28] Serra wanted priests who would work hard and who could cope with the difficulties that were certain to occur.

CHAPTER SEVEN

MORE MISSIONS, MORE PROBLEMS

 Although he never gave up and always worked toward achieving his goal, to build the chain of missions, Father Serra spent many hours trying to improve relations with the Native Americans and to resolve church-military conflicts.

Relations with the Native Americans were particularly bad at the San Diego de Alcalá mission. After Father Serra left for Monterey, Father Luis was made mission head. Later, the mission was relocated to a new site, farther away from the presidio and near a Native American village. There, the missionaries built a church, housing for the Native Americans, and other

Mission San Diego de Alcalá was moved to its present site in 1774. This is the first mission founded by Father Serra. Father Luis Jaime is buried under the mission's church.

buildings.[1] By October 1775, they had converted five hundred Native Americans, but their success did not last.

On November 5, 1775, there was a major setback, a Native American attack. Three men were killed, including Father Luis, and the mission was burned. Father Serra ordered it to be rebuilt. After a new church had been built, as well as the other buildings that were needed, an adobe wall was built around the entire area for protection. Although there continued to be difficulties with the Native Americans, the mission succeeded.[2]

The San Diego mission did well, but Father Serra still had conflicts with the military. Some of the highest-ranking military leaders disliked the fathers and their work. These leaders thought that the fathers were too kind to the Native Americans, that too much money was being spent on the missions, and that not enough was going to the military. Also, some army leaders wanted to use their posts to make money. A few cheated and stole from their own men. Some also took mission supplies.

In addition, many soldiers mistreated the Native Americans, especially the women. Some of the soldiers who had been released from Spanish prisons and forced into army service, raped Native American women and beat up the Native American men who tried to defend them. If they caught Native Americans stealing, they would beat or kill them.

While the soldiers treated the Native Americans cruelly, Father Serra and the other missionaries were trying to gain their friendship. They wanted them to live on the mission grounds so they could better teach them about the Roman Catholic religion as well as about Spanish customs. The soldiers' brutal actions made the fathers' jobs much more difficult.

Father Serra had great trouble dealing with the Monterey-Carmel area military chief, Pedro Fages, who was in charge of the northern California area. Fages was a cruel man who treated his own men terribly. In one report that an officer sent to the viceroy, it was charged that Fages beat his men and officers with a club and forced them to buy his goods at triple the value. Fages cut their rations in half while the food rotted in storage. The officer wrote, "We had to live on rats, coyotes, vipers [snakes], crows, and generally every creature that moved on the earth . . . to keep from starvation."[3]

He also made life for Father Serra and the other fathers miserable. Father Serra wrote, "How many times I have thought that his bullyings would end by being the death of me!"[4]

This situation was one of the reasons that Father Serra asked for permission to move the Monterey and San Diego missions to new locations.[5]

Finally, Father Serra decided that he had to talk to the viceroy, Antonio Bucareli. To do this, he traveled more than two thousand miles to Mexico City. When they met and Serra told Bucareli what had happened, the viceroy asked him to put this report in writing. The report that Father Serra sent to the viceroy from Alta California was called *Representación*. It was, in effect, a Bill of Rights for the Native Americans: ". . . it formed the basis for the first significant legislation for early California."[6]

The viceroy, impressed with Father Serra's knowledge, met with his officials and examined the report. He granted most of Father Serra's requests.

The viceroy issued orders that included removing Fages and appointing a new leader, who was told to give the fathers more help. The viceroy also gave the fathers more control over the Native Americans. He ordered that the baptized Native Americans' government, religious training, and general education be under missionary supervision.[7]

Another major area covered in the viceroy's order dealt with the Spanish soldiers. To end the conflicts, the viceroy made many new rules, most of which covered the soldiers' problems. He said that the soldiers would be paid more so that they could buy what they wanted instead of stealing. Married soldiers who served in California would be allowed to visit their families. New soldiers who were sent to California and who were married could bring their families with them. Soldiers who married Native American women would be given money. One important rule that Father Serra welcomed was that soldiers who abused Native Americans would be removed from their jobs.

The viceroy's orders greatly pleased Father Serra. As a result, he was able to improve mission conditions. Although there were still problems, he made a good deal of progress.

The viceroy also had given his approval to start more missions. These missions would be built near the ocean so they easily could receive their supplies from

Spanish ships. The two missions that had already been built, one in the North and one in the South, were near good ports. Because of their success, the Spanish government made plans to develop the San Francisco Bay area, which had good harbors. This was especially important because settlement there could prevent enemy attacks.

The third mission, San Antonio de Padua was founded on July 14, 1771. It was named by the viceroy, after San Antonio, one of Father Serra's favorite saints, who had lived in Italy in the 1200s.[8] The San Antonio de Padua mission was built at a site in the Santa Lucía Mountains.

After Father Serra arrived to start the San Antonio mission, he raised a wooden cross and held services. Native Americans were attracted to the mission through gifts of glass beads and other goods. In return, the Native Americans gave the Spaniards nuts and seeds. Father Serra was pleased with the start of the mission. He stayed there for about two weeks and then returned to Carmel.

Two priests were placed in charge of San Antonio. One of them, Father Buenaventura Sitjar, served the mission for thirty-seven years. He was one of the people who recommended that the San Antonio mission, like the others, be moved to another location. This was done in 1773. He also made many improvements to the mission. The most important was bringing water to the mission from the nearby San Antonio River through the use of dams and aqueducts. On the fertile soil, the mission grew enough wheat to feed everyone who lived there.[9]

Father Sitjar also helped the mission in other ways. To work more effectively with the Native Americans, whose language (Mutsun) the fathers did not understand, he wrote a four-hundred-page Mutsun language-Spanish dictionary, as well as other books. Father Sitjar's work enabled the fathers to translate Roman Catholic prayers into Mutsun. This helped the Native Americans learn more quickly about the Roman Catholic religion.[10]

The fourth mission, San Gabriel Arcángel, was founded on September 8, 1771, on the banks of the Río de los Temblores (River of the Earthquakes), now called the San Gabriel River. A flash flood wiped out the first crops, and the mission was moved to a safer location, five miles away. Mission San Gabriel was built about nine miles east of present-day Los Angeles. Located in a fertile area, it soon became one of the most productive missions.[11]

Although it grew a great deal of food, the San Gabriel mission had terrible relations with Native Americans because the Spanish soldiers treated them so badly. In fact, the mission almost suffered an attack after a soldier raped the local Native American chief's wife. When the chief, with a large group of his warriors, attacked the soldier and tried to kill him, another soldier shot the chief. The fathers prevented a Native American attack on the mission when they forced the San Gabriel military leader to exile the soldier.[12]

Even after the viceroy's orders, Father Serra still had trouble with the Alta governor, who was also the chief military leader. After the San Diego Native American attack, the governor would not allow Father Serra to go there for many months. He may have thought that Father Serra would travel from San Diego to Mexico City, where he could again tell the viceroy about all that had happened recently.[13]

Father Serra also worried about the Spanish military reaction to Native American attacks. He was afraid that if the soldiers were ordered to kill Native Americans, the Native Americans would die without converting, which meant that they could not go to heaven. This would also delay more mission-building.

Father Serra wrote to the viceroy, especially about the San Diego de Alcalá attack and asked that the jailed Native Americans be treated leniently. The viceroy took Father Serra's advice, and one of the Native American leaders of the San Diego revolt, after being in prison for a short time, was released.

Meanwhile, another mission was built. In the Valley of the Bears, the fifth mission, named for its large number of bears, was built. The mission, San Luis Obispo de Tolosa, was founded on September 1, 1772.[14]

It was named for a Franciscan saint, San Luis (St. Louis), who was a French bishop. Father Serra raised the cross, blessed the new mission, and held services. Father José Cavaller was placed in charge of the mission.

At San Luis Obispo, Father Serra and the others watched the "spouting of whales" and, saw "dolphins or tunny fish, sea otter and sea lions."[15]

The new mission had good luck. A supply ship that had been delayed arrived with the needed building materials. With the materials, they built a chapel, warehouse, and housing for the priests and soldiers. The buildings were made of wood, with roofs made of rushes. The mission produced wines, olive oil, vegetables, and fruits.

Hostile Native Americans attacked the mission three times between 1772 and 1774. These attacks were not as serious as the one at San Diego, but the roofs of the buildings caught fire, and the mission had to be rebuilt. Tile roofs were built to replace the straw ones for this mission and the others.[16]

After this, four more missions were founded: San Francisco de Asís on June 29, 1776; San Juan Capistrano on November 1, 1776; Santa Clara de Asís on January 12, 1777; and finally, the long-delayed San Buenaventura on March 31, 1782. Towns developed where some of the missions had been built. These included San Diego, Carmel, Monterey, San José, and San Francisco.

The exterior of the church at Mission Santa Bárbara was based on a Roman design. The town of Santa Bárbara, California, orginated because of this mission.

The founding of San Francisco and Monterey was different from what had happened in other places. To ensure the success of the missions and their presidios, the viceroy ordered that families be brought in. He ordered the explorer Juan Bautista de Anza to find safe trails over which the settlers could travel and to bring families to northern California through these trails. In a group, they would travel from Mexico to California. The settlers would first stay in the area's mission, and then build a town.[17]

On one of the trips, Anza brought to Monterey two hundred forty colonists and soldiers with their families. They had with them about a thousand animals, including cattle and horses. They traveled for six months; during the trip, four children were born.[18]

In the North, Anza picked a site for another presidio and a mission. He turned it over to Father Palóu and to a Spanish leader, Lieutenant Gabriel Morago. Twenty-five families settled there near a river, Arroyo de los Dolores (Stream of the Sorrows). Today, the mission is often called Mission Dolores instead of its full name, San Francisco de Asís. It was started in October 1776.[19]

When Father Serra and Inspector-General Gálvez had made their early plans to build the missions, Gálvez said, "If St. Francis desires a mission, let him show us his harbor and he shall have one."[20] After the harbor was found, the Spanish government approved the plans to build a mission there. Once they were ready to start building it, Father Serra arrived. He dedicated it to St. Francis, the Franciscan founder. The settlers, soldiers, fathers, and a few Native Americans had a feast. They paraded through the area with a statue of St. Francis, and then placed the statue on the altar. To celebrate, the new colonists sang, and the soldiers shot cannons.[21] Father Pedro Font described it:

> . . . although in my travels I saw very good sites and beautiful country, I saw none which pleased me so much as this. And I think if it could be well settled like Europe there would not be anything more beautiful in all the world, for it has the best advantages for founding in it a most beautiful city, with all the conveniences desired by land as well as by sea.[22]

Father Serra and the others who were there could not know that their tiny settlement would develop into one of the largest and most important American Pacific Coast cities—San Francisco.

Even though he had successfully started so many missions, all the recent political and military conflicts resulted in Father Serra losing his position as mission president for a short time. A few months later, he was renamed to the job.

Although his left foot and leg infections got worse, Father Serra decided that he needed to visit the missions. The four-month trip was hard for him, but it was a success. After he returned to Carmel, he wrote,

"I was completely worn out during my extensive journey, but I encountered no mishap or adverse effects, thanks be to God."[23]

He also had to deal with a new military leader, Governor Felipe de Neve, who questioned Father Serra's right to perform confirmations. Confirmation is an important step in becoming a Roman Catholic; it takes place a certain time after the new convert has been baptized. Usually, only bishops (high church officials) have the right to confirm. However, because the missions had no bishop over them, Father Serra had asked for the right to confirm. This had been granted, in 1774, by the Pope (the head of the Roman Catholic Church), who gave Father Serra the power to confirm for a ten-year period only.

With this new power, Father Serra planned to make a confirmation tour of the eight missions. He would travel to San Diego by sea on the *Santiago*, then travel north, stopping at each mission along the way. Father Serra left on August 24 and reached San Diego on September 15, planning to start the confirmations right away.

When Governor Neve heard about Father Serra's confirmation trip, he demanded that Father Serra give to him the original document that had been issued by the Pope. Father Serra could not do that, because he had only a copy of it. While he sent for the original document, he decided to start his confirmation tour. If

Governor Neve wanted to punish him, he would just have to take his chances.

His goal was to confirm "everybody from San Diego to San Antonio." He reached a total of 1,716 Native American confirmees. Once he returned to Carmel, he said that he was "entirely worn out."[24]

Although Governor Neve was very upset that Father Serra had disobeyed his orders, he decided not to punish him. The viceroy had sent him word that Father Serra had the power to confirm. Also, the governor needed Father Serra and the other fathers to run the missions and to build more. Father Serra was relieved by the governor's decision.

In the meantime, Father Serra was given good news. He found out that Monterey had been made the Alta California capital. To Father Serra, it meant that the Spanish government honored the work that he and the other fathers had done. He wrote about the joy he felt as a result of Monterey becoming the capital.[25]

While he was waiting to start the San Buenaventura mission, Father Serra turned his attention to planning a new mission at Santa Barbara. He thought that the governor had given him permission by telling him to go there. Once he reached the area, he was told not to build a mission, but instead to start a military chapel for the presidio. Discouraged, he finished the work at Santa Barbara and then returned to Carmel.

In 1782, part of Father Serra's long-awaited goal, to build more missions along the Santa Barbara Channel, came true. He and the other fathers had planned to build three missions between San Gabriel and San Luis Obispo. The missions would be named San Buenaventura, Santa Bárbara, and La Purísima Concepción.

Father Serra had longed to found more missions in the area because of the large number of Chumash who lived there.

The Chumash were skilled at making canoes and baskets. They farmed, fished, and traded with other people who lived on the nearby islands. When Father Serra was told that at least one mission could be built in the area he said, "I saw those inhabitants [the Chumash] as I had always seen them, lively, agreeable, and . . . asking for the light of the Gospel."[26]

The first mission to be built along the channel was San Buenaventura. It would be located at Mitz-kana-kan, a Native American town of five hundred people.[27] Father Palóu, who was familiar with the area, had told Father Serra that there were thousands of possible Native American converts.

Leading a group that included soldiers as well as the governor, Father Serra arrived at the site where the mission would be built. On Easter Sunday, in 1782, services were held, and the new mission-to-be was blessed. For the feast that followed, a bull was killed. This was eaten by the soldiers and the rest of the group, but the fathers, instead of eating the bull, ate lamb. Killing and eating a lamb on Easter Sunday was an old Mallorcan custom.[28] After the feast ended, with Native American help, Father Serra and his companions started building the mission.

The San Buenaventura mission was named for John Fidanza, who lived in Italy during the 1200s. The name San Buenaventura came from an event that happened when Fidanza, as a child, had become very sick and was near death. He prayed that his life be spared. St. Francis, who was at his bedside, added his own prayers. Suddenly, Fidanza got better. He stood up and said that he was cured. When this happened, St. Francis cried, *"O buona ventura!"* ("Oh what good fortune!") After that, the boy was called Buona Ventura (in Spanish, Buenaventura). He became a Franciscan and rose to a high position in the order. He is regarded as the Franciscans' second founder.

The San Buenaventura mission, like the others, had its share of problems, including a major earthquake in 1812, in which it was destroyed. It was rebuilt and the mission proved to be successful.

Father Serra did not know that the San Buenaventura mission would be the last one that he would start. The Alta California military commander, Fernando de Rivera, was not an admirer of the

Mission San Buenaventura was founded in 1782. The mission, dedicated on Easter Sunday, was located in an area that had a large Native American population. Mission San Buenaventura was the last mission Father Serra founded.

mission movement. Despite orders from the viceroy to continue building missions, Rivera delayed as long as possible. The viceroy's lack of action meant that Father Serra was unable to found Santa Barbara. It was built after his death by the mission president who replaced him. Although Father Serra was heartbroken that he could not start new missions, he spent the rest of his remaining years helping those that had already been established.

MISSION LIFE

 Father Serra, in a letter to the viceroy, wrote about the need to continue the mission system:

> [Missions], will not only provide it with what is most important . . . the Holy Gospel . . . but also will be the means of supplying foodstuffs. . . . They will accomplish this far more efficiently than these pueblos without priests.[1]

There had been a plan to start more California towns including one in Los Angeles, but Father Serra was against it. He thought that the towns, which would have no priests, would develop into places of sin. He was afraid "that they would be prejudicial to Indian and mission rights."[2] Despite Father Serra's feelings about the towns, the Spanish government decided to start them.

Father Serra and the church favored missions over towns because they felt that missions were the best way to spread Roman Catholicism. The Spanish government agreed that missions were important, but it had political and economic goals that were thought to be just as important as religious ones. Towns would be a good place for Spanish people to settle, and they would insure that the region had a stable government. More important, the presence of Spanish colonists would keep other countries from moving onto Spanish lands. It also was thought that towns would provide an important base for the nearby farming areas. The towns would have governments that could settle arguments as well as shops that could sell needed goods.

In spite of the government's plan, for a few years Father Serra and the church managed to keep the Spanish officials convinced that the best way to settle California was through the mission system. Government officials agreed because missions could be started with little money. To provide the missions with the supplies and other needed things, they could use money from the Pious Fund. This fund came from money taken from the Jesuits who had been forced out of Baja California. The fund also used donations to start and support the missions. Most of the donations had been given by people who lived in Mexico. Since the Pious Fund was run by the church, the government did not need to spend much money on the missions.[3]

Once the missions had been built, they could, within a certain period of time, grow enough food to feed the people who lived on the mission grounds. Another advantage was that fewer soldiers would have to be sent into Alta California to control the Native Americans. The fathers would work with the Native Americans to teach them how to be "good Christians," which they thought would keep the Native Americans peaceful.

The overall plan was that the missions would only last a short time; then the missionaries were expected to leave and go to other areas. Legally, ten years was the time set aside for the missions to do their work. After that, the natives would be "civilized" enough to run a pueblo by themselves. In some areas, such as Mexico, Central America, and Peru, this had happened.

In California, because the Native American culture was so different from that of the Spanish, the "civilization plan" did not work. The Native Americans who lived in the California missions were not allowed to manage their own affairs for a long time. Even after sixty-five years of missionary control, when the order came to turn the missions into towns, the expected

Native American control of the towns did not happen.[4]

The fathers were not entirely at fault. Even though the fathers had planned to learn the Native Americans' languages and then use these languages when they taught, they were not able to do it. There were too many languages to learn. If the fathers could not speak with the Native Americans, they could not teach them.

Also, the Spanish language and the Native Americans' languages were very different. The Native Americans had few words for ideas or beliefs; most of the Native American words were based on things that could be seen, heard, touched, or tasted. Faced with these problems, Father Serra and the other missionaries had to change their plan. They decided that instead of the missionaries learning the Native American languages, the Native Americans would have to learn Spanish. Then they could all speak with and understand each other. Teaching the Native Americans Spanish took longer than they had expected.

Education was another problem. The fathers thought that the Native Americans could gain from formal schooling. They were taught subjects that students learned in Spanish schools, such as arithmetic, writing, and reading. Some students also learned Latin, the language which is used for Roman Catholic prayers. The fathers found that most of the

Native Americans could not master these subjects quickly. Instead, the fathers taught them skills that they thought were needed to survive in Spanish culture: farming, carpentry, sewing, and metal working. In California, training rarely went beyond basic skills. The largest schools that taught skills had more than two thousand Native American students.[5]

Life in most of the missions was the same everywhere. It was based on a daily schedule that the fathers worked out and enforced. In one mission, San Diego de Alcalá, the normal routine was based on teaching the Native Americans who lived there "everyday religious, social, moral, and industrial practices."[6]

The day's routine was almost always the same. In the morning, the fathers would hold services and give the Native Americans religious training. They would then all sit down to have breakfast. The day's work consisted of the men working in the fields and the women making soap, baskets, and other needed goods. The women were also taught sewing so that they could make the Native Americans' clothing, but in Spanish style.[7]

The routine continued into the evening. At night, the Native Americans were again taught religion. They were also taught the Spanish language. Before they went to bed, they were usually given about one hour to relax. The women went to sleep at 8:00 P.M. and the men at 9:00 P.M. Sometimes there might be a

The dining room at Mission San Carlos de Borromeo de Carmelo. In 1794, over nine hundred Native Americans lived at the mission.

fiesta with dancing and games—the Native Americans loved these activities. Fiestas were the only break in the daily mission schedule.[8]

Although the missionaries emphasized religion, the Spanish language, and skills, they also taught the Native Americans about Spanish art and music. Some of the Native Americans' paintings, such as those from San Juan Capistrano, became famous. Since many Native Americans enjoyed Spanish music, the fathers organized them into bands and orchestras. One Native

American musical group was known throughout the coast.[9]

While they taught them skills, the fathers also tried to change the Native Americans' customs, especially in regard to marriage. The fathers disliked the customs that let Native American men marry more than one wife and divorce.[10] They made the mission Native Americans agree to lifelong marriage with only one spouse. The fathers also tried to change the practice of Native American men marrying sisters, and even the sisters' mother, a practice which kept families together. The fathers wrote about a man who had married several sisters: "When baptized, he put them all away except the oldest sister who had been his first choice; while the others, being also baptized, were married to baptized men according to the . . . ritual."[11]

The missionaries encouraged the Spanish soldiers to marry Native American women legally. Marriage between soldiers and Native Americans would lead to the spread of Roman Catholicism.[12]

A French sailor who visited the California missions was impressed by many of the things that he saw. He thought the mission system was much kinder to the Native Americans than the ways that the soldiers and colonists of other countries had treated Native Americans in other areas. On visits to other parts of the Americas, he had seen Native Americans killed and beaten.

The sailor also noted that the missions controlled Native Americans' property but did not take it away from them. This, he wrote, was not a problem for the Native Americans, since they did not have a custom of one-person land ownership. He also thought that the Spanish custom of letting Native American *alcaldes* (mayors) and *caciques* (leaders) act as justices of the peace to settle problems was a good one. These Native American leaders were elected by their own people. Although they made some decisions about matters that affected Native American life, the fathers had to approve most of their decisions. If not, the Native American leaders would not be allowed to carry them out.[13]

To govern the missions, the fathers had many rules. Most of these rules had come from the Spanish government and from Franciscan church officials. The missions were so far away from the places where the officials worked that sometimes it would take months, or even years, to get answers to their questions, or even the final permission to start a mission.

Once permission to start a mission was given, the mission president, Father Serra, would select two fathers to run it. One of the two was made the local mission head. Father Serra thought that there were advantages to having two fathers posted at each mission: The fathers could divide up the work. Also, having two instead of one at each mission, especially in the first years, kept them from being lonely. Even with this practice, some missionaries could not handle the stress or hard conditions.

The missions had similar buildings that were built in a certain style: Each was a large four-sided building that was built around a square courtyard. In some cases, the mission was spread out over more than six acres. The inner side of the square had rooms that were used for workshops, priests' quarters, eating and cooking, storage, and offices. There also were separate areas for unmarried Native American women. After they married, couples were given other rooms.

The most important mission building was, of course, the church, which always was built first. The design of the churches, on the outside and on the inside, was similar to that of Spanish churches. In the mission interiors, Native American design still can be seen.[14] The fathers held services in the churches for the Native Americans. Later, the Spanish settlers who had started ranches and towns attended.

There were only one or two doors on the outside of each mission complex building. These doors were locked at night to protect the people who were inside as well as to make certain that the Native Americans would not leave during the night. If they tried to leave, "they were hunted down, and, if captured, brought back and punished."[15] With all these rules in force, the mission Native Americans led a controlled life of hard work.

100

Some historians think that the mission system treated the Native Americans harshly and that mission life for the Native Americans was a disaster. They give many reasons to support their views. First, the Native Americans were infected with diseases that they got from the soldiers and the missionaries. The Native Americans had no natural immunity to the white men's sicknesses, and because of this, they died by the thousands.

Second, some people think that the fathers should not have tried to change the Native Americans' customs and tried to make them into Spaniards. Before the fathers arrived in California and started the missions, the Native Americans had lived very well. They had enough food, they practiced their own customs, and they were healthy. After the missions were built and the Native Americans moved into them, Native American culture was destroyed.

Another point of view, held by other historians, is that the Native Americans were much better off after the missions were started. They stress how well the fathers treated them. The fathers were kind to the Native Americans, and they helped them lead a "better" life. They protected the Native Americans from the bad things that had happened to Native Americans in non-Spanish areas. This included whites giving the Native Americans liquor, ignoring their education, taking their land, and forcing them onto reservations. In California, the fathers taught them the Roman Catholic religion, gave them education, taught them skills, and tried to help them get used to a much different way of life than the one that they were used to.

More important, these historians think that the missions provided a peaceful way of settling new, Spanish-owned lands. The mission Native Americans who adopted the new ways were given land to farm. The argument that supports the fathers' work with the Native Americans can be summarized in this quotation, written by a Roman Catholic Church official:

> The old Spanish system was one of wisdom and showed a better understanding of Native American psychology . . . than any other system even devised for the . . . guidance of a race. That a handful of missionaries with a few soldiers and artisans could set up in the wilderness the three institutions for Spanish conquest of presidio, pueblo, and church and have them remain . . . as agencies for good is almost beyond our comprehension.[16]

However, another author has written, "From an Indian point of view, the introduction of the mission system meant cultural and physical genocide."[17] Genocide occurs when one group of people destroys another group out of hatred for its culture, race, or religion.

FATHER SERRA'S DEATH

 In 1784, Father Serra went on his last trip on behalf of the missions. He left Carmel to start a northern confirmation tour. He had severe chest pains and his leg and foot were so swollen that his group brought along a litter (a covered couch) for him to ride in. He refused to use it and said, "I shall be looking on it from the outside . . . the Governor['s] . . . wife . . . will be the one to occupy the inside."[1] For most of the trip, he rode a mule.

During the trip, he also dedicated Mission Santa Clara de Asís's new church. He was happy that a new church had been built, but he was saddened that

Father José Murguía, the mission's cofounder, had died suddenly. While he was at Santa Clara, Father Serra also told Father Palóu good-bye. Father Serra was certain that because of his age and health problems he would soon die.

By the time Father Serra returned to Carmel, he was very ill. In August 1784, during the last three weeks of his life, Father Serra tried to finish his last tasks. He wrote farewell letters to the fathers who served the missions, and he asked them to visit him. When Father Palóu came to see him, he was shocked by how sick Father Serra looked.

No matter how sick he was, Father Serra refused to stay in bed; he did his normal jobs. One day, Father Palóu was surprised to hear him singing in the chapel, and he told a soldier who was there, "It does not seem that the Father-president is very sick." The soldier said to him, "Father, there is no basis for hope. He is ill . . . [He] is always well when it comes to praying and singing, but he is nearly finished."[2]

During the next few days, Father Serra's health got worse. He had trouble breathing, and his leg was swollen—he knew that he was dying. Although he was near death, he talked to Father Palóu about the success of the California missions.

He recounted what the fathers had been able to accomplish. During the fifteen years in which the nine missions had been built, the Spanish had started to

CALIFORNIA MISSIONS

San Francisco de Asís
• Santa Clara de Asís

• San Carlos Borromeo de Carmelo
• San Antonio de Padua

• San Luis Obispo de Tolosa

• San Buenaventura
• San Gabriel Arcángel
• San Juan Capistrano
San Diego de Alcalá

Father Serra founded nine missions along the coast of California.

settle in California. The founding of the missions had kept other countries from claiming the land. There were now more than a thousand colonists, a few presidios, and some towns. The missions were doing well and they were reaching their main goal: to convert the Native Americans.

Still, Father Serra was worried about the missions. Americans were beginning to enter California from the west. More important, there was a rumor that the Spanish government would take the missions away from the Franciscans and give them to the Dominicans, another religious order. (This never happened, and the Franciscans kept control.) People who had heard the rumor asked Father Serra if it was true. He did not know the answer.

As Father Serra's sickness got worse, word spread that he was dying. When the *San Carlos* reached Monterey, the ship's doctor came to examine him. Dr. Juan García tried to ease his breathing by applying extreme heat to his chest. This did not help at all—it only gave Father Serra more pain.[3]

Although Father Serra was sick, he still kept his sense of humor. Father Palóu later wrote an amusing story about the "chicken woman," who appeared while he was visiting Father Serra. One day, Father Palóu and Father Serra were sitting outside the mission church when an old Native American woman walked up to them. They had called her the chicken woman when, about ten years earlier, she had come to the mission looking for chickens to eat. She killed and ate the few chickens that were there. The fathers had been upset because they had so few chickens to start with. Now, they had even fewer.[4]

Father Serra had forgiven the old woman a long time ago. She was back, and this time, instead of chickens, she wanted something to keep her warm at night. She told them that she always got cold. Father Serra got up and went to his room. When he returned, he was carrying half of a blanket. Father Serra had taken his only blanket, cut it in half, and brought the old woman the other half. This made the chicken woman very happy. After she left, Father Serra and Father Palóu laughed at the old chicken story. At least this time she had not killed any more mission animals![5]

While they sat and talked, Fathers Serra and Palóu discussed mission problems, especially the need for more Spanish priests. Father Serra suggested that Father Crespí's diaries, which were at the College of San Fernando, be published. Father Palóu decided that Father Serra's own story would be the best way to interest more fathers in California mission work. Later, he wrote a book about Father Serra's life.[6]

Father Palóu's book, *Vida del Padre Junípero Serra* (The Life of Father Junípero Serra), was published in Mexico City, three years after Father

Serra's death. This book was widely read and it made Father Serra a hero of "legendary fame."[7]

Knowing that the end was near, Father Serra ordered the mission carpenter to build him a coffin.

In spite of his sickness, Father Serra felt a little better when he learned that the officers of the *San Carlos* had come to see him. To honor them, he had the mission bells rung. He greeted them warmly and listened to their stories about their trips to Peru. He gave them no sign that he was gravely ill, but he knew that he would not see them again.

On August 28, his breathing got much worse. He said to Father Palóu, "It is siesta time. Now let us go to rest."[8] He lay down on his bed and fell asleep. Later, when Father Palóu checked to see how he was doing, he discovered that Father Serra had died in his sleep.

Father Serra's death was greatly mourned. Church bells were rung, and cannons were fired. Crying Native Americans from miles around the mission came to pay their respects. Although there were soldiers guarding Father Serra's body, some of the Native Americans cut off small pieces of his robe and hair as mementoes.[9]

Father Palóu wrote about how people reacted to Father Serra's death: "As soon as the . . . [bells] rang out the sad news, the whole town assembled, weeping over the death of their beloved father . . . So great was the crowd of people, including Indians and soldiers and sailors, that it was necessary to close the door."[10]

Father Serra was buried on August 29, 1784. Father Palóu held the funeral services. About six hundred Native Americans from nearby areas were there. Father Serra was buried in the church floor, next to Father Juan Crespí. Father Palóu, Father Serra's closest friend, knew that a great man had died.

Father Palóu gave Father Serra's handkerchief to Dr. Juan García, the doctor who had attended Father Serra when he was sick. The doctor said that "with this little cloth, I expect to effect more cures than with all my books and pharmacy."[11] The doctor was convinced that Father Serra was such a holy man that anything associated with him would make people believe they could be cured.

After Father Serra's death, the College of San Fernando picked a new mission president. For a few months, Father Palóu held the post, but it was not the kind of work that he wanted to do. Father Palóu wanted to retire in Mexico City and write a book about Father Serra's life. The college agreed to let him leave and picked Father Fermín Francisco de Lasuén as the official president. Father Lasuén had served at missions San Gabriel, San Diego, and San Carlos.[12]

Father Lasuén proved to be an able leader. He managed to get along with the governors and the soldiers. He continued the custom of the mission

San Luis Rey de Francia was built in 1798. It was the last mission founded by Father Lasuén.

president's living at the San Carlos Borromeo mission, where the records for all the missions were kept. It also had a library with more than twenty-five hundred books. Missionaries and suppilies were sent to San Carlos from Mexico.[13]

Before Father Lasuén died in 1803, he founded nine more missions: Santa Bárbara, 1786; La Purísima Concepción, 1787; Santa Cruz, 1791; Nuestra Señora de la Soledad, 1791; San José, 1797; San Juan Bautista, 1797; San Miguel Arcángel, 1797; San Fernando Rey de España, 1797; and San Luis Rey de Francia, 1798.

In addition to building more missions, Father Lasuén doubled the number of converts. He also improved the mission farms and industries. He was also responsible for what is now called mission-style architecture, which used tile and stone, or adobe, for building materials. Father Lasuén built the new missions in this style and then had the old ones rebuilt the same way.

After Father Lasuén's death, three more missions were built: Santa Inés, 1804; San Rafael Arcángel, 1817; and the northernmost mission, San Francicso Solano, 1823. San Francisco Solano was named for the saint who had been a missionary to Native Americans of Peru. He had been a saint whom Father Serra greatly admired.

FATHER SERRA'S LEGACY

The mission system started to fall apart after Mexico became independent from Spain in 1821. The new Mexican government gave the Native Americans in California citizenship, but this made little difference. The mission Native Americans continued to live in the missions, the same way they had done while the missions were under Spanish control.

The missions ended in the 1830s when the Mexican government passed a law that turned the missions into pueblos and the Native Americans were given land legally. All Spanish-born priests were expelled. Mexican settlers were able to buy Native American land. Often, instead of buying it, the settlers just took it and "the Indians lost everything."[1]

When this new policy went into effect, many Native Americans left the missions and moved to towns such as Los Angeles and San José. Some worked as farmhands and *vaqueros* (cowboys), for California ranchers. Few Native Americans returned to their old tribal ways.

The end of the missions had a terrible effect on the lives of the mission Native Americans. They were so used to mission life that most of them ended up working for the new landowners, who mainly were interested in the cheap labor that the Native Americans provided. Many landowners treated these people like slaves. Even the few Native Americans who owned land lost it when the new settlers found ways to take it from them legally. After a few years, the California Native Americans were a minority in their own land.

In 1845, the Mexican governor of California, Pío Pico, put the missions up for sale. The final blow came in 1849, when the United States defeated Mexico in the Mexican War (1848–1849). After the Treaty of Guadalupe Hidalgo was signed at the end the war, the United States gained millions of acres of Mexican land. This land included what had been called Alta California—the Americans called it California. United

The Junípero Serra Museum is located on Presidio Hill in San Diego, California. Built in 1929, the museum contains items from the 1700s.

States control ended what was left of the old mission system. Without the needed upkeep, most of the mission buildings started to decay.

In the 1900s, there was renewed interest in preserving and restoring the missions. In the 1920s and 1930s, most of the missions were restored. Today, thousands of visitors from all over the United States, as well as from other countries, visit them to enjoy their beauty and history. One author summarizes their influence: ". . . the missions have enriched California and even the nation to a degree that, given their unpromising beginnings, would have astonished their Spanish founders."[2]

Father Serra's achievements were amazing. The others who followed him in mission-building were successful, but it was Father Serra who started the "golden mission" chain. In addition to founding missions, presidios, and towns, Father Serra achieved a record number of religious deeds. He baptized thousands of Native Americans, introduced the Roman Catholic religion into California, and taught the natives about European culture. Many West Coast cities developed from missions or presidios, among them San Diego, Los Angeles, San José, San Francisco, and Carmel.

Father Serra has been honored for his many achievements. Throughout California, there are many Father Serra statues. The most visited of these is the one in Sacramento, the state capital. The most famous statue is in Washington, D.C., in Statuary Hall, in the U.S. Capitol Building. In this hall, each state has placed statues of its two most important people.

In the 1920s, the United States government asked California to pick two people to be honored. There was a great deal of debate over who the two should be. What helped the state officials decide was a 1921 San Francisco newspaper poll. Out of one hundred people, the newspaper's readers picked Father Serra as one of their two top choices.[3] California selected Father Serra as one of the two; the other one is of Thomas Starr King, a California minister.

In 1931, the two statues were finished, sent to Washington D.C., and placed in Statuary Hall. They were accepted by an act of Congress.

In addition to these statues, there are many buildings and places named for Father Serra. The buildings include the Junípero Serra Museum (San Diego), the Serra State Building (Los Angeles), and the Serra Memorial Hospital (Los Angeles). There are so many California streets and highways named after Father Serra that it is impossible to list them all. In addition, there was a United States ship, the *SS Junípero Serra*, and at least one railroad station.

Some people consider Father Serra's achievements so outstanding that they want to do even more to honor him. A few are working to get the Roman Catholic Church to recognize him as an official saint. One author has written, "Serra . . . will always be the Serra of the history books and the Serra of household phrase. But once he is given the honor of the altar he would be officially called . . . Saint Junípero."[4]

Although Father Serra died before the entire chain of missions was built, his impact on California has never ended. He left a continuing legacy that includes much of California's progress, especially in its ranches and farms. Many of its important crops, such as

The gardens at Mission San Diego de Alcalá are still used today. Many of California's first crops were originally grown in the mission gardens.

artichokes, olives, almonds, figs, oranges, apricots, and grapes, were planted first in mission gardens and orchards. Father Serra also taught California's first farmers, the Native Americans, how to grow desert crops. This was done by irrigation, bringing water from rivers and lakes into dry areas.

Another contribution was the road that was used to travel the miles between the missions. It was called *El Camino Reál* (The Royal Highway). It was California's first road, and it is still used today. U.S. Highway 101 follows most of the old mission road.

Each year, thousands of people visit the missions, many of which are now church-owned. Most of the missions have been rebuilt and restored. The visitors are impressed by their history, their beauty, and their peacefulness. Some missions are museums, but many also have active churches. Several are Franciscan monasteries. Two are used as centers for higher education.

The missions are considered to be an important part of California's past, but few people know the full story of the missions' founding. It was all because of the stubborn father whose favorite saying was to "always go forward, and never turn back."

CHRONOLOGY

1713— Miguel José Serra is born on November 24 in Petra, Mallorca.

1729—Miguel José enters the Franciscan religious order.

1737— Miguel José becomes a priest and changes his name to Father Junípero Serra.

1749—Father Serra travels to Spain and then to Mexico.

1767—Father Serra is named superior of the Franciscan missions in Baja California.

1769—Father Serra founds San Diego de Alcalá.

1770—Father Serra founds San Carlos Borromeo de Carmelo.

1771— Father Serra founds San Antonio de Padua and San Gabriel Arcángel.

1772—Father Serra founds San Luis Obispo de Tolosa.

1776—Father Serra founds San Francisco de Asís (Mission Dolores) and San Juan Capistrano.

1777— Father Serra founds Santa Clara de Asís.

1782—Father Serra founds San Buenaventura.

1784—Father Serra dies on August 28 in Carmel, California.

1821—Mexico gains independence from Spain, and the mission system in California declines.

1833—The Mexican government turns the California missions into pueblos and expells all Spanish-born priests.

CHAPTER NOTES

CHAPTER 1

1. Donald DeNevi and Noel Francis Moholy, *Junípero Serra* (New York: Harper & Row Publishers, 1985), p. 150.

2. Daniel Fogel, *Junípero Serra, The Vatican, and Enslavement Theology* (San Francisco: Ism Press, 1988), p. 63.

3. I. Brent Eagen, *A History of Mission Basílica San Diego de Alcalá, The First Church of California Founded by the Venerable Junípero Serra* (San Diego: Mission Basílica San Diego de Alcalá), pp. 5, 6.

4. Winifred I. Wise, *Fray Junípero Serra and the California Conquest* (New York: Charles Scribner's Sons, 1967), p. 117.

CHAPTER 2

1. Donald DeNevi and Noel Francis Moholy, *Junípero Serra* (New York: Harper & Row Publishers, 1985), p. 12.

2. Omer Englebert, *The Last of the Conquistadors: Junípero Serra* (Westport, Conn.: Greenwood Press Publishers, 1956), pp. 3, 4.

3. DeNevi and Moholy, p. 13.

4. Kathleen Allan Meyer, *Father Serra: Traveler on the Golden Chain* (Huntington, Ind.: Our Sunday Visitor Publishing Division, 1990), p. 3.

5. Ibid., p. 1.

6. Ibid., pp. 1, 2.

7. Meyer, p. 7.

8. Ibid., p. 6.

9. DeNevi and Moholy, p. 7.

10. As cited in Martin J. Morgado, *Junípero Serra's Legacy* (Pacific Grove, Calif.: Mount Carmel, 1987), p. 4.

11. Marion F. Sullivan, *Westward the Bells: A Biography of Junípero Serra* (Boston: St. Paul Books & Media, 1988), p. 15.

12. Francis J. Weber, *A Bicentennial Compendium of Maynard J. Geiger's The Life and Times of Fray Junípero Serra* (San Luis Obispo, Calif.: EZ Nature Books, 1984), p. 4.

13. Englebert, p. 7.

14. Sullivan, pp. 31–32.

15. Morgado, p. 5.

16. Sullivan, p. 21.

CHAPTER 3

1. Martin J. Morgado, *Junípero Serra's Legacy* (Pacific Grove, Calif.: Mount Carmel, 1987), p. 6.

2. Donald DeNevi and Noel Francis Moholy, *Junípero Serra* (New York: Harper & Row Publishers, 1985), pp. 35–36.

3. Omer Englebert, *The Last of the Conquistadors: Junípero Serra* (Westport, Conn.: Greenwood Press Publishers, 1956), pp. 3, 4.

4. Ibid., p. 13.

5. Winifred I. Wise, *Fray Junípero Serra and the California Conquest* (New York: Charles Scribner's Sons, 1967), pp. 9–10.

6. Morgado, p. 6.

7. Englebert, pp. 14–16.

8. Wise, p. 12.

9. Englebert, p. 17.

10. Ibid.

11. Wise, p. 13.

12. Thomas F. Cullen, *The Spirit of Serra* (North Providence, R.I.: The Franciscan Missionaries of Mary, 1935), p. 25.

13. Ibid. p. 24.

CHAPTER 4

1. Donald DeNevi and Francis Moholy, *Junípero Serra* (New York: Harper & Row Publishers, 1985), p. 44.

2. Thomas F. Cullen, *The Spirit of Serra* (North Providence, R.I.: The Franciscan Missionaries of Mary, 1935), p. 36.

3. Daniel Fogel, *Junípero Serra, The Vatican, and Enslavement Theology* (San Francisco: Ism Press, 1988), p. 43.

4. Omer Englebert, *The Last of the Conquistadors: Junípero Serra* (Westport, Conn.: Greenwood Press Publishers, 1956), p. 39.

5. Marion F. Sullivan, *Westward the Bells: A Biography of Junípero Serra* (Boston: St. Paul Books & Media, 1988), p. 49.

6. Winifred I. Wise, *Fray Junípero Serra and the California Conquest* (New York: Charles Scribner's Sons, 1967), p. 17.

7. Martin J. Morgado, *Junípero Serra's Legacy* (Pacific Grove, Calif.: Mount Carmel, 1987), p. 13.

8. DeNevi and Moholy, p. 55.

9. Ibid., pp. 55–56.

10. Fogel, p. 45.

11. DeNevi and Moholy, pp. 57–58.

12. Englebert, p. 46.

13. DeNevi and Moholy, pp. 57, 58.

14. Englebert, p. 48.

15. Francis J. Weber, *A Bicentennial Compendium of Maynard J. Geiger's The Life and Times of Fray Junípero Serra* (Mission Hills, Calif.: EZ Nature Books, 1984), p. 16.

16. Wise, p. 22.

17. Ibid.
18. DeNevi and Moholy, p. 6.
19. Ibid., pp. 66–67.

CHAPTER 5

1. Agnes Repplier, *Junípero Serra: Pioneer Colonist of California* (Garden City, N.Y.: Doubleday, Doran & Company, 1933), pp. 9–10.

2. I. Brent Eagen, *A History of Mission Basílica San Diego de Alcalá, the First Church of California Founded by the Venerable Junípero Serra* (San Diego: Mission Basílica Dan Diego de Alcalá), pp. 5, 6.

3. Repplier, pp. 10, 12.

4. Ibid., p. 47.

5. Daniel Fogel, *Junípero Serra, The Vatican, and Enslavement Theology* (San Francisco: Ism Press, 1988), p. 83.

6. Linda Lingheim, *The Native Americans and the California Missions* (Van Nuys, Calif.: Langtry Publications, 1990), pp. 15, 16–18.

7. Fogel, p. 91.

8. Sunset Editors, *The California Missions: A Pictorial History* (Menlo Park, Calif.: Sunset Publishing Corporation, 1993), p. 51.

9. Ibid.

10. Ibid.

11. Ibid.

12. Lingheim, pp. 17, 18.

13. Fogel, p. 93.

14. Ibid., pp. 94–95.

15. Ibid.

16. Fogel, p. 97.

17. Ibid.

18. Lingheim, p. 22.

CHAPTER 6

1. Donald DeNevi and Noel Francis Moholy, *Junípero Serra* (San Francisco: Harper & Row Publishers, 1985), p. 69.

2. Daniel Fogel, *Junípero Serra, The Vatican, and Enslavement Theology* (San Francisco: Ism Press, 1988), pp. 50, 51.

3. Winifred E. Wise, *Fray Junípero Serra and the California Conquest* (New York: Charles Scribner's Sons, 1967), p. 31.

4. Marion F. Sullivan, *Westward the Bells: A Biography of Junípero Serra* (Boston: St. Paul Books & Media, 1988), pp. 64–68.

5. Wise, p. 80.

6. Agnes Repplier, *Junípero Serra: Pioneer Colonist of California* (Garden City, N.Y.: Doubleday, Doran & Company, 1933), p. 59.

7. Omer Englebert, *The Last of the Conquistadors: Junípero Serra* (Westport, Conn.: Greenwood Press Publishers, 1956), p. 72.

8. Repplier, p. 65.

9. DeNevi and Moholy, p. 21.

10. Martin J. Morgado, *Junípero Serra's Legacy* (Pacific Grove, Calif.: Mount Carmel, 1987), p. 33.

11. Ibid., p. 34.

12. Ibid., pp. 31–32.

13. DeNevi and Moholy, p. 87.

14. Sunset Editors, *The California Missions: A Pictorial History* (Menlo Park, Calif.: Sunset Publishing Corporation, 1993), pp. 40, 41.

15. Richard Pourade, *The History of San Diego; The Explorers* (San Diego: Union-Tribune Publishing Company, 1960), p. 104.

16. Sunset Editors, p. 40.

17. I. Brent Eagen, *A History of Mission Basílica San Diego de Alcalá, The First Church of California Founded by the Venerable Junípero Serra* (San Diego: Mission Basilica San Diego de Alcalá), pp. 3, 4.

18. Sullivan, p. 81.

19. Eagen, p. 3.

20. Sullivan, p. 83.

21. Ibid.

22. Ibid.

23. Wise, p. 43.

24. Repplier, pp. 74–75.

25. Wise, p. 61.

26. Sullivan, p. 84.

27. Ibid., p. 87.

28. Francis J. Weber, *A Bicentennial Compendium of Maynard J. Geiger's The Life and Times of Fray Junípero Serra* (Mission Hills, Calif.: EZ Nature Books, 1984), p. 28.

CHAPTER 7

1. I. Brent Eagen, *A History of Mission Basílica San Diego de Alcalá, the First Church of California Founded by the Venerable Junípero Serra* (San Diego: Mission Basílica San Diego de Alcalá), p. 4.

2. Ibid., pp. 5, 6.

3. Omer Englebert, *The Last of the Conquistadors: Junípero Serra* (Westport, Conn.: Greenwood Press, Publishers, 1956), pp. 92, 93.

4. Ibid., p. 93.

5. Francis J. Weber, *A Bicentennial Compendium of Maynard J. Geiger's The Life and Times of Fray Junípero Serra* (Mission Hills, Calif.: EZ Nature Books, 1984), pp. 35–38.

6. Ibid., p. 37.

7. Ibid., pp. 37–38.

8. Sunset Editors, *The California Missions: A Pictorial History* (Menlo Park, Calif.: Sunset Publishing Corporation, 1993), p. 308.

9. Stanley Young, *The Missions of California* (San Francisco: Chronicle Books, 1988), p. 77.

10. Sunset Editors, p. 102.

11. Young, p. 31.

12. Richard B. Wright, ed., *California's Missions* (Arroyo Grande, Calif.: Hilbert A. Lowman, 1978), p. 25.

13. Donald DeNevi and Francis Moholy, *Junípero Serra* (New York: Harper & Row Publishers, 1985), p. 163.

14. Wright, p. 29.

15. Winifred I. Wise, *Fray Junípero Serra and the California Conquest* (New York: Charles Scribner's Sons, 1967), p. 125.

16. Wright, p. 29.

17. Kathleen Allan Meyer, *Father Serra: Traveler on the Golden Chain* (Huntington, Ind.: Our Sunday Visitor Publishing Division, 1990), p. 42.

18. Ibid.

19. Ibid.

20. Sunset Editors, p. 125.

21. Meyer, p. 42.

22. Weber, p. 59.

23. DeNevi and Moholy, p. 179.

24. Martin J. Morgado, *Junípero Serra's Legacy* (Pacific Grove, Calif.: Mount Carmel, 1987), p. 80.

25. Wise, p. 140.

26. DeNevi and Moholy, p. 189.

27. Young, p. 45.

28. Morgado, p. 86.

CHAPTER 8

1. Winifred I. Wise, *Fray Junípero Serra and the California Conquest* (New York: Charles Scribner's Sons, 1967), p. 150.

2. Francis J. Weber, *A Bicentennial Compendium of Maynard J. Geiger's The Life and Times of Fray Junípero Serra* (Mission Hills, Calif.: EZ Nature Books, 1984), p. 73.

3. Omer Englebert, *The Last of the Conquistadors: Junípero Serra* (Westport, Conn.: Greenwood Press Publishers, 1956), pp. 59, 60.

4. Sunset Editors, *The California Missions: A Pictorial History* (Menlo Park, Calif.: Sunset Publishing Corporation, 1993), pp. 53, 54.

5. Ibid. p. 56.

6. I. Brent Eagen, *A History of Mission Basílica San Diego de Alcalá, the First Church of California Founded by the Venerable Junípero Serra* (San Diego: Mission Basílica San Diego de Alcalá), p. 8.

7. Ibid.

8. Ibid.

9. Thomas F. Cullen, *The Spirit of Serra* (North Providence, R.I.: The Franciscan Missionaries of Mary, 1935), p. 157.

10. Wise, pp. 138–139.

11. Agnes Repplier, *Junípero Serra: Pioneer Colonist of California* (Garden City, N.Y.: Doubleday, Doran & Company, 1933), p. 200.

12. Wise, p. 139.

13. Repplier, p. 203.

14. Stanley Young, *The Missions of California* (San Francisco: Chronicle Books, 1988), p. 7.

15. Ibid. p. 6.

16. Cullen, p. 160.

17. Young, p. 6.

CHAPTER 9

1. Martin J. Morgado, *Junípero Serra's Legacy* (Pacific Grove, Calif.: Mount Carmel, 1987), p. 88.

2. Marion F. Sullivan, *Westward the Bells: A Biography of Junípero Serra* (Boston: St. Paul Books & Media, 1988), p. 151.

3. Ibid.

4. Kathleen Allan Meyer, *Father Serra: Traveler on the Golden Chain* (Huntington, Ind.: Our Sunday Visitor Publishing Division, 1990), p. 52.

5. Sullivan, pp. 151, 152.

6. Donald DeNevi and Noel Francis Moholy, *Junípero Serra* (New York: Harper & Row Publishers, 1985), p. 202.

7. John A. Berger, *The Franciscan Missions of California* (New York: G.P. Putnam's Sons, 1941), p. 342.

8. Meyer, pp. 52, 53.

9. Ibid. p. 53.

10. Winifred I. Wise, *Fray Junípero Serra and the California Conquest* (New York: Charles Scribner's Sons, 1967), p. 160.

11. Francis J. Weber, *A Bicentennial Compendium of Maynard J. Geiger's The Life and Times of Fray Junípero Serra* (Mission Hills, Calif.: EZ Nature Books, 1984), p. 84.

12. Berger, p. 274.

13. Ibid.

CHAPTER 10

1. Stanley Young, *The Missions of California* (San Francisco: Chronicle Books, 1988), p. 7.

2. Ibid. p. 3.

3. Martin J. Morgado, *Junípero Serra's Legacy* (Pacific Grove, Calif.: Mount Carmel, 1987), p. 92.

4. Ibid.

FURTHER READING

Berger, John A. *The Franciscan Missions of California*. New York: G.P. Putnam's Sons, 1941.

DeNevi, Donald and Noel Francis Moholy. *Junípero Serra*. New York: Harper & Row Publishers, 1985.

Fogel, Daniel. *Junípero Serra, The Vatican, and Enslavement Theology*. San Francisco: Ism Press, 1988.

Lingheim, Linda. *The Native Americans and the California Missions*. Van Nuys, Calif.: Langtry Publications, 1990.

Meyer, Kathleen Allan. *Father Serra: Traveler on the Golden Chain*. Huntington, Ind.: Our Sunday Visitor Publishing Division, 1990.

Morgado, Martin J. *Junípero Serra's Legacy*. Pacific Grove, Calif.: Mount Carmel, 1987.

Repplier, Agnes. *Junípero Serra: Pioneer Colonist of California*. Garden City, N.Y.: Doubleday, Doran & Company, 1933.

Sullivan, Marion J. *Westward the Bells: A Biography of Junípero Serra*. Boston: St. Paul Books & Media, 1985.

Sunset Editors. *The California Missions: A Pictorial History*. Menlo Park, Calif.: Sunset Publishing Corporation, 1993.

Weber, Francis J. *A Bicentennial Compendium of Maynard J. Geiger's The Life and Times of Fray Junípero Serra*. Mission Hills, Calif.: EZ Nature Books, 1984.

Wright, Richard B., ed. *California's Missions*. Arroyo Grande, Calif.: Hilbert A. Lowman, 1978.

Young, Stanley. *The Missions of California*. San Francisco: Chronicle Books, 1988.

Video—*Inside the California Missions*. Santa Barbara, Calif.: Cultural Videos, 1992.

Slides & Cassette—*The Story of the California Missions*. Whitter, Calif.: Finley Holiday Film Corporation.

INDEX

Cat in a
Red Hot
Rage

* These are the reissued editions.
† Also mystery

Cat in a Red Hot Rage

A MIDNIGHT LOUIE MYSTERY

Carole Nelson Douglas

A Tom Doherty Associates Book
New York

CAT IN A RED HOT RAGE: A MIDNIGHT LOUIE MYSTERY

This book is printed on acid-free paper.

A Forge Book
Published by Tom Doherty Associates, LLC
175 Fifth Avenue
New York, NY 10010

www.tor.com

Forge® is a registered trademark of Tom Doherty Associates, LLC.

Library of Congress Cataloging-in-Publication Data

Douglas, Carole Nelson.
Cat in a red hot rage : a Midnight Louie mystery / Carole Nelson Douglas.
p. cm.
"A Tom Doherty Associates Book."
ISBN-13: 978-0-765-31401-7
ISBN-10: 0-765-31401-0
1. Midnight Louie (Fictitious character)—Fiction.   2. Barr, Temple (Fictitious character)—Fiction.   3. Public relations consultants—Fiction.   4. Women cat owners—Fiction.   5. Cats—Fiction. Las Vegas (Nev.)—Fiction. I. Title.
PS3554.O8237 C27695 2007
813'.54—dc22

2006102854

First Edition: May 2007

Printed in the United States of America

0   9   8   7   6   5   4   3   2   1

For all the women whose zest for life and spirit of
survival and sisterhood never fades at any age,
whether they wear pink ribbons or red hats
or their hearts on their sleeves

Contents